Temple Bar

THE POWER OF AN IDEA

TEMPLE BAR PROPERTIES LIMITED
1996

THE POWER OF AN IDEA
TEMPLE BAR

Published to coincide with the completion
of Phase 1 of the development of Temple
Bar, July 1996

ISBN   1-874202-09-5

Editor   Patricia Quinn

TEMPLE BAR PROPERTIES LIMITED
18 Eustace Street, Temple Bar, Dublin 2
tel: 01-6772255 / fax: 01-6772525
e-mail: tbp@iol.ie

Produced for Temple Bar Properties by
Gandon Editions, Oysterhaven, Kinsale
tel 021-770830 / fax 021-770755

Design   John O'Regan
              (© Gandon, 1996)
Production   Nicola Dearey, Gandon
Photography   credits at end of book
Printing   Betaprint, Dublin

cover   Meeting House Square
              (film show, June 1996)

frontispiece Aerial view of Temple Bar

THIS PROJECT HAS BEEN
PART-FINANCED BY THE
EUROPEAN REGIONAL
DEVELOPMENT FUND

DEPARTMENT OF THE
ENVIRONMENT

Foreword

THE REVITALISATION OF TEMPLE BAR HAS BEEN BROUGHT ABOUT IN A WAY WHICH respects and reinforces the cultural tradition and heritage of the area. This has been achieved by ensuring that physical regeneration and the development of cultural facilities to occupy the new or refurbished buildings have gone hand in hand. After decades of quiet decline and slow decay, more recent years have seen a vibrant renewal of the area. Exciting architectural forms are appearing. New buildings neatly inserted into the existing street patterns are adding life and activity to the urban scene that is Temple Bar.

Temple Bar is the natural home for Dublin's Cultural Quarter. The area is culturally rich in the sense that it has a highly distinctive historical, architectural and archaeological heritage. The indigenous cultural base there has now been expanded and forms the key to the area's regeneration. An architectural competition held by Temple Bar Properties resulted in an overall framework plan for Temple Bar. This in turn set the parameters for a development programme of cultural, leisure, small business and residential uses for the company's properties.

Public art has also established a strong tradition in Temple Bar. On any casual ramble, artistic expression is evident on the streets with many examples of unique street furniture which combine practical uses and artistic design. There is also much evidence of artistic expression in the buildings themselves, including motifs, specially designed entrances, etc. Artists and architects have clearly collaborated closely in bringing these unique features to the streets and buildings of the area.

Resolving the environmental problems associated with urban life and promoting the green agenda in the urban context have featured strongly in the overall programme. The innovative and integrated approach taken sets a headline for urban renewal elsewhere.

The cultural and indeed economic life of the centre of Dublin has expanded tremendously since Dublin's designation as European City of Culture in 1991. The revitalisation of Temple Bar has made no small contribution to establishing Dublin as a city which can stand comparison with any other European capital. Phase 1 is now completed, and Temple Bar Properties are embarking on the second phase of this exciting and innovative rejuvenation. Posterity will have to judge the success of the Temple Bar project in the longer term. For one contemporary view, I can do no better than quote the leading British architect Ted Cullinan, who described Temple Bar recently as 'one of the best urban renewal projects in Europe'.

BRENDAN HOWLIN TD
Minister for the Environment

Contents

Temple Bar in Transition

THE IMPORTANCE OF RECORDING CONTEMPORARY COMMENT ON URBAN INTERVENTIONS was demonstrated in the recent French architectural exhibition, *The Metamorphosis of Paris*, which showed how leading intellectuals of the day, such as Victor Hugo and Guy de Maupassant, bemoaned the newly erected Eiffel Tower, just as Dublin City Councillors of their day called for the Ha'penny Bridge to be removed because they considered it so unsightly. There has been a great deal of comment on the Temple Bar redevelopment, some positive, some negative. It will be interesting for future generations to read this book, giving as it does an overview of the state of renewal of the area as it was in 1996. As David Mackay in his essay observes, that which is cherished creates passionate interest, which explains in part why this small area of some twenty-eight acres in the heart of Dublin has been the subject of so much attention. It would seem that the very idea of Temple Bar has caught the public's imagination. While there are many aspects of the renewal programme, it was the idea of Temple Bar as Dublin's Cultural Quarter that most encouraged its supporters.

This renewal programme is complex, in physical layout, in building stock, in delivery mechanisms, in financing, in uses. Each part of the programme is complex in its own way. Temple Bar is one of the most historically, architecturally and archaeologically rich areas of the city, yet the programme operates within the bounds of the 1991 Temple Bar Architectural Framework Plan. The treatment of the building stock varies from total conservation to total replacement, with all shades of adaptation in between. The public-private sector delivery mechanism results from an imaginative community proposal to save the area from being turned into a vast bus station and instead to develop it as a Cultural Quarter; the public sector further defined the redevelopment proposal, and the private sector operated within that framework. To quote John Mulcahy: 'To harness market forces to non-market ends, you must embark on a highly interventionist approach.'

The financing has been equally complex, involving a combination of private and public funding. There is a broad mix of uses of the area – in the private sector, apartments, shops, hotels, bars, etc, and, in the public sector, cultural centres, streetscape improvement schemes, and the Green Building. The programme is aimed at catering for local residents, for Dubliners in general, and, of course, for foreign visitors. The provision of facilities for this mixed group has been undertaken with respect for the existing building stock and taking into account financial and heritage constraints, but it is the cultural aspect that has been of paramount concern in the development.

There are substantial challenges when culture is used to spearhead an urban renewal project: the 'gentrification' of other areas is well documented. The proposal to concentrate on culture in the Temple Bar project originally came from Temple Bar's own cultural community, who, fed up with leaking roofs and having seen the uncertainty which was created by earlier proposals for the area, seized the opportunity to propose permanent homes in Temple Bar for their organisations. Specifically, Project Arts Centre, the Gallery of Photography, the Irish Film Centre, Temple Lane Studios and Temple Bar Gallery and Studios sought to improve their lot and the lot of other cultural providers in the area. These bodies (with the exception of Project Arts Centre, the scheme for which is in the planning stages) have had their buildings redeveloped through the use of European and Irish public funds, and their futures are now secure. In addition, new multi-media, children's arts, and design centres are also in place. Paradoxically, the fact that proposals which originated from the cultural community have been realised has given rise to unease within that community about the dangers posed to artistic creativity by State intervention. By stating that 'where the infrastructure is in place one expects better delivery of the finished artistic project', Colm Ó Briain has pointed to a challenge facing the Temple Bar cultural community, which is as significant in its way as the threat of a bus station obliterating the area.

Other conflicts, or apparent conflicts, will be influential in the future of Temple Bar, and these must be taken account of in any analysis of the redevelopment. I believe that there is a creative tension between apparently conflicting uses and users of the area – for example, residents and publicans, commercial and not-for-profit enterprise, culture and tourism – which will in fact ensure the sustainability of the area. A kind of 'area democracy' will, I believe, maintain a balance, whereby one sector will not prevail over another. Temple Bar has always been about contradiction and multiple uses, and the area is robust enough to sustain a high level of apparent conflict.

I began by saying that, as in the case of Paris, future generations would be interested to compare their evaluation of Temple Bar with contemporary opinions and commentaries, like those recorded in this book. However, Temple Bar is more than a series of discrete projects, and the fact that the overall project of renewal is still incomplete makes it very difficult to form a comprehensive judgement. In any event, Temple Bar will never be 'finished'; like Paris, it will continue to metamorphose over time as new uses place different demands on the existing framework of buildings. What does merit comment at this stage in the process is the fact that Phase 1 of a concerted intervention of the State has been brought to completion: a concentrated, time-based, area-based and finance-based intervention towards the achievement of one powerful idea – the realisation of Temple Bar as Dublin's Cultural Quarter. Phase 2, which will take us up to the millennium, is about to begin.

LAURA MAGAHY
Managing Director
Temple Bar Properties

Introduction

THIS BOOK HAS BEEN PREPARED AS PART OF THE CELEBRATION OF THE COMPLETION OF Phase 1 of the Temple Bar urban renewal project, 1991-1996. Phase 1 has involved the processes of analysis and consultation, design and construction, and the inhabitation of new buildings by residents, retailers, artists and cultural organisations. The idea of a publication to mark this intensive activity is to give some insight into the nature of the processes involved, and to offer an opportunity to various commentators to give their view on the value of the enterprise at this interim stage. We have asked a broad range of experts in different fields to comment on the project from many different perspectives. The diversity of their views and the different values which they place on individual aspects of the project reflect the mixture of agendas and special interests which characterise Temple Bar itself. They have been given very little editorial direction, beyond a request to address themselves to the general reader.

As well as including specialised insights from commentators, we have asked Group 91 Architects to revisit their original urban framework plan for Temple Bar, reflecting not just on the developments achieved, but also on those which fell by the wayside. It might appear in retrospect that all of the elements of the Temple Bar Development Programme were preordained and self-evident, but, in fact, the project involved an enormous amount of learning and creative invention, as well as experience and professional expertise.

Because of their importance as a collective infrastructural investment, all of the completed cultural projects have been described in some detail, both by their designers and by the directors of the organisations who now manage them. We have also included a number of examples of commercial projects, both by Temple Bar Properties and the private sector, in order to illustrate the range of schemes which form part of the entire project. An inventory of all of the developments undertaken in Temple Bar since 1991 is provided for reference purposes, as is an inventory of all of the works – temporary or otherwise – commissioned from visual artists by Temple Bar Properties.

It will be clear that the Temple Bar project is a large and ambitious one. Perhaps it is not an exaggeration to describe it as a *grand projet* in the European sense. It is perhaps now possible to see, in the material presented here, that much of the energy and imagination which has driven the individual elements has derived from the collective vision of the project as a whole. This is certainly a case of the whole being greater than the sum of its parts, and it is to be hoped that this synergy will continue to find expression in the life and work of the population of residents, artists and traders who use the buildings in the future.

ACKNOWLEDGEMENTS

Very many individuals have contributed to the projects described in this book. For reasons of space, we have adopted the convention whereby only the architect is given the credit for a building, which means that all of the other members of the design team, as well as the specialist consultants from all fields, the contractors and their myriad of sub-contractors, are not listed.

In the production of the book, we have been greatly facilitated by the promptness and co-operation of the contributors, whether essayists, end-users or architects, and I would like to express my grateful appreciation to all of them. We are particularly indebted to the photographers, whose images do so much to communicate the variety and richness of the project, and I would like to add my personal thanks to my colleague Paul O'Shea, for his inexhaustible patience in assembling this comprehensive photographic record.

Finally, this opportunity must be taken to pay tribute to John O'Regan and Nicola Dearey of Gandon Editions, who have, in the space of ten years, transformed the climate for the dissemination of criticism and commentary on the visual and plastic arts in Ireland, and who brought to this publication all of their customary care, diligence and skill.

PATRICIA QUINN
Cultural Director
Temple Bar Properties

Essays

The community origins of the Temple Bar project

JOHN QUILLINAN AND RICHARD WENTGES

SINCE 1991, THE TEMPLE BAR AREA HAS BEEN TRANSFORMED FROM RELATIVE OBSCURITY into one of the most complex and ambitious urban regeneration projects since the foundation of the State. Temple Bar is a phenomenon that has been heavily marketed and widely discussed in the media, to the extent that the general public is now generally aware of its location, identity and characteristics. Yet it was not always so.

Ten years ago, most people if presented with the name Temple Bar would have assumed that it referred to a public house. In this paper, we discuss the dynamics underlying Temple Bar's transformation from relative obscurity in 1986 to the £100 million urban renewal programme that was launched in 1991. The magnitude of this transformation poses, to our way of thinking, a number of questions:

- what created the original identity of the area?
- how and why did the idea of a development come about?
- how was the idea transformed into the current development process?

Our approach in answering these questions, as two people who were actively involved in the area during the period in question, is necessarily from a historical perspective, but is not intended to be a comprehensive history of the road to the development.

By way of conclusion, we consider whether there are any elements or methodology in that process that could be used as models for similar redevelopments elsewhere.

Crown Alley, with Merchants Arch in the distance (1991)

opposite
The former clothing factory in which Temple Bar Gallery and Studios started out in 1983

TOWARDS AN IDENTITY

The boundaries of the area that we now know as Temple Bar – defined by the Temple Bar Area Renewal and Development Act (1991) – are Westmoreland Street and the Civic Offices to the east and west, and Dame Street and the Liffey quays to the south and north. In the early 1980s, however, the words Temple Bar only signified the name of a small street running through the centre of the area, a public house of the same name, and a building housing artists' studios and a gallery. The central core of the area had been, since 1966, designated as the site for Córas Iompair Éireann's new transportation centre. The substance of this proposal was the provision of a city bus station connected by underground rail links to Heuston and Connolly stations. It was to be built on interconnected sites on both sides of the Liffey.

Since 1981, CIÉ had been assembling the site for this development by purchasing property as it became available. The long-term aim was to demolish the existing buildings on these properties to facilitate the proposed transportation centre development. In the interim, CIÉ agreed to let these premises on short term leases and low rents. This attracted a number of temporary tenants engaged in a range of diverse activities. As time passed, these tenants began to feel less temporary as they started to identify with the area, and, through their activities and businesses, they created an identity for it. The threat of the ultimate destruction of the area created a sense of solidarity among these tenants and reinforced the identity that was emerging. By 1987, many of the tenants were considering methods of protecting their future in Temple Bar, and were discussing among themselves how security of tenure might be achieved.

The first use of the expression 'the Temple Bar area' that appeared in print was in An Taisce's 1985 report, *The Temple Bar Area – A Policy for its Future*. Similarly alerted by the threat to the historic streets and buildings of the area which the proposed transportation centre presented, An Taisce recognised the physical identity of the area and its potential for sensitive redevelopment. Soon after the publication of this report, the media started to refer to the threatened site as the Temple Bar area, while those living and working in the area were quick to adopt the title as a symbol of their identity.

IDEAS FOR DEVELOPMENT

The An Taisce report focused its attention primarily on the desirability of conserving the significant historic streets and buildings in Temple Bar. It is noteworthy that the report suggested that the area be designated for special tax incentives to facilitate refurbishment of the older building stock. An Taisce also concluded that Temple Bar had the potential to become Dublin's Latin Quarter.

The establishment of the Project Arts Centre and the Irish Film Centre in premises which they had purchased, and Temple Bar Gallery and Studios, the Gallery of Photography, and a number of individual artists in CIÉ buildings, began to give the area a cultural identity upon which these locally based cultural bodies were anxious to build. The larger organisations formed the Temple Bar Study Group, and proposed a redevelopment of the area with a strong emphasis on the development of existing cultural activities. The establishment on Temple Lane of recording and rehearsal studios for emerging contemporary musicians broadened the cultural base of Temple Bar and started to attract more of the younger generation into the area.

Meanwhile, in Crown Alley and Merchants Arch, a number of small retailers had established alternative fashion outlets. Furthermore, with the redevelopment of a privately owned furniture warehouse into retail outlets, this busy pedestrian link between the north- and south-city shopping areas quickly became established as a centre for alternative youth culture. The Crown Alley experience provided a vibrant image of Temple Bar, both for the general public and for the people working in the area. It was soon being cited as a possible model for the redevelopment of adjacent streets. The establishment of a number of new restaurants in the area further broadened the base of Temple Bar's diversity of users. Together with the pubs, which had already become popular with people working in the area, these restaurants began to create an ambience which hinted at how the area might become a centre for city night-culture.

Temple Bar only had a small residential population (just under 200 people), mainly living in private rented accommodation. As older tenants on fixed rents passed away or moved out, landlords in the area were not slow in re-letting their properties at current market rents. The enthusiasm that many of the new residents showed for their new homes soon began to convince like-minded people that not only could they survive in the inner city, but that there were also significant advantages in doing so.

Despite the fact that Dublin Corporation's Draft Dublin City Development Plan supported the transportation centre, in 1989 its Paving Section completely restored the stone setts and granite paving on Temple Lane. This was welcomed by the people of Temple Bar as an indication that the Corporation recognised the value of the historic fabric of the area.

THE IDEAS COME TOGETHER

Temple Bar Development Council

The fact that many of the new activities that had established themselves in Temple Bar were operating in CIÉ buildings on short-term leases without any security of tenure was jeopardising their future development. Many found themselves unable to enter into arrangements with financial institutions,

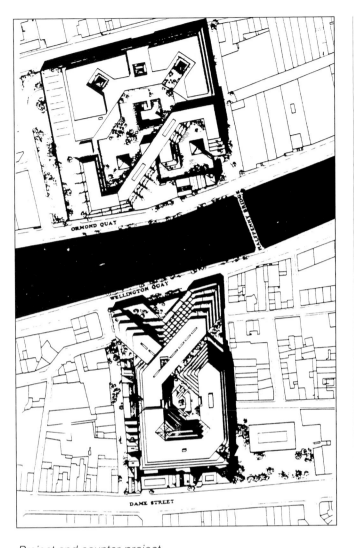

Project and counter-project
above – Map showing the extent of the proposed
transportation centre
below – An alternative approach (Temple Bar Study', 1986)

as they did not possess the necessary property title. The Dublin Resource Centre (DRC), a co-operative on Crow Street, was investigating ways of improving this situation when it became obvious that in order to achieve security of tenure, they would first have to defeat the prime cause of their insecurity – the plans for the transportation centre.

It was decided by the DRC to call a public meeting with an agenda that focused on opposing the transportation centre's inclusion in Dublin Corporation's Draft Dublin City Development Plan. Other CIÉ tenants, such as Temple Lane Studios, Temple Bar Gallery and Studios and the Gallery of Photography, as well as a number of retailers who were similarly affected, were quick to support this initiative. The meeting also attracted the support of bodies which, although not directly threatened (the Irish Film Institute, the Project Arts Centre, the Crown Alley traders and a number of residents), felt that their future in the area would be significantly impaired by the establishment of the transportation centre. The meeting was addressed by members of the media and An Taisce, who, while supportive of the initiative, expressed the view that opposition to the transportation centre alone would not constitute a significantly powerful platform, and that positive proposals for the redevelopment of the area should also be included.

That was the week that was, April 22-29, 1988

The meeting was faced with the problem that only one week remained before the deadline for submissions to the Corporation's Draft Dublin City Development Plan. Accordingly, a committee of six was elected from among the 75-100 people present to draw up development proposals for the submission. There followed a week of frantic work during which the committee met every day. The title of 'Temple Bar Development Council' was chosen as a name which reflected the coming together of the people of the area with a common identity and common goals. Many sources and resources were drawn upon to devise a set of proposals which would achieve a broad measure of support. The meeting reconvened at the end of the week to examine the proposals put forward by the committee, which were adopted as the Temple Bar Development Council's submission to the Draft Development Plan. Once the Council had been established and the submission made to Dublin Corporation, the proposals for the development of Temple Bar entered the public domain.

The Development Council's submission sought to enlist the support of Dublin Corporation in the following ways:

1 to disallow any proposal for a CIÉ transportation centre from being included in the Development Plan
2 to draw up a local area action plan which would facilitate the rejuvenation of the Temple Bar area
3 to upgrade the streets with paving, pedestrianisation, landscaping, lighting, etc
4 to offer tax incentives specifically directed to encourage

the refurbishment of existing buildings and the suitable development of infill sites

5 to act upon the An Taisce recommendations regarding the listing of buildings in the Temple Bar area

6 to assist in creating a central, attractive business and residential area providing ongoing employment and residences for Dublin people

7 to establish Temple Bar as the cultural centre of the city and as a major tourist attraction

The recommendations of this submission were to remain the platform from which the Development Council lobbied local and central government representatives over the next three years, and went on to form the basis of the framework for the eventual redevelopment.

The Development Council committee defended their submission at an oral hearing in Dublin Corporation's Planning Department in October 1988. Following this meeting, and also following discussions with the Assistant City Manager's office and other relevant Dublin Corporation departments, it was clear to the members of the committee that there was considerable support within the Corporation for the proposals being put forward by the Development Council. The committee felt sufficiently encouraged to present their proposals to the Department of the Environment and also to the Department of the Taoiseach.

THE POWER OF AN IDEA

Subsequent to the oral hearing on the submission to Dublin Corporation, it became evident to the members of the Temple Bar Development Council that their development proposals were powerful enough to meet a receptive response from those agencies charged with the development of the city. In our view, there were a number of factors that contributed to this receptiveness.

Since the mid-seventies, there had been a shift in attitude as to what constituted good urban planning and development. There was a growing acknowledgement in planning circles that the planning policies of the sixties and seventies, coupled with the speculative development of the city centre, had failed to deliver an urban environment of sufficient quality to respond to the needs and aspirations of the capital city's population. There was new thinking about alternative models for urban regeneration. Ever since the Council of Europe's 'Declaration of Amsterdam', to which Ireland was a signatory, the importance of conserving architectural and civic heritage had been gaining momentum.

A clear indication of the extent to which Dublin Corporation's thinking had changed was evidenced by the publication in 1990 of Dublin Corporation Planning Department's Area Action Plan for Temple Bar. This examined the physical, land-use and socio-economic features of the area, analysed the strengths and weaknesses, and proposed policies, specific controls and specific objectives for the future development of the area.

At the same time there emerged a new public sense of ownership of the city. Public involvement in conservation and anti-development campaigns, such as Wood Quay and the battles to save Hume Street and Lower Fitzwilliam Street, together with the media coverage of these events, helped heighten public consciousness about urban planning issues.

The proposals that Temple Bar Development Council submitted to Dublin Corporation were powerful enough to win general approval for a number of reasons. The transportation centre was presented as an essentially formless yet threatening monolith that would destroy everything that Temple Bar was starting to become. The rest of the Temple Bar Development Council proposals were short, simple and easily understood. Their appeal was sufficiently broad and inclusive to enlist the support of all the activists in the area. Perhaps, most importantly, the proposals focused on specific actions that needed to be taken.

The seven proposals, outlined earlier, addressed themselves to the following civic/governmental agencies respectively:

1 CIÉ
2 Dublin Corporation Planning Department
3 Dublin Corporation Paving Department
4 Department of Finance
5 Dublin Corporation Planning Department
6 Department of Trade and Tourism/Bord Fáilte
7 Department of the Taoiseach (Arts and Culture)

It soon became evident that co-ordinating the actions and securing the co-operation of so many civic and governmental departments would be impossible without direct government intervention.

As early as 1987, the Taoiseach of the day, Charles J Haughey, had stated publicly: 'Temple Bar is one of the most important, traditional, attractive and noteworthy parts of the city, and it has to be refurbished and kept, and I won't let CIÉ near it.' Encouraged by this expression of interest, the Temple Bar Development Council felt confident enough to approach the Department of the Taoiseach directly with their proposals. It is significant that the Department of the Taoiseach held the Arts and Culture portfolio at this time, and that the Structural Funds of the EU represented a major potential source of funding for infrastructural projects. Up to one third of the property in the Temple Bar area was in public ownership, either by CIÉ, Dublin Corporation, Telecom Eireann or the ESB. The Department of the Taoiseach was in a uniquely powerful position to facilitate the purchase of certain of these properties for the development.

Temple Bar, furthermore, provided an eminently suitable flagship project for Dublin's year as European City of Culture in 1991, and received Urban Pilot Project funding on this basis, following a submission by Dublin Corporation and Temple Bar '91, a locally based consortium of developers. The direct interest and subsequent intense involvement by the Department of the Taoiseach was undoubtedly one of the most important factors in translating the Temple Bar Development Council's proposals into a viable redevelopment package. It is arguable that only the centralised power of the Taoiseach's office could have co-ordinated the necessary responses from the various civic and governmental agencies listed above, and ultimately bring forward the enabling legislation that allowed the development to proceed.

CONCLUSION

At various stages in the formulation of policy by the Temple Bar Development Council, there was an acute awareness of Temple Bar's location in the heart of the capital city and the need to ensure that whatever development took place should be exemplary, and hopefully serve as a model for similar developments elsewhere. Whereas, in our opinion, a number of factors that led to Temple Bar's development were unique to the area, there are a number of essential elements which might be helpful to any group contemplating a similar type of development.

1 Identity – The easy identification factor is of primary importance. Whatever project is envisaged, its location needs to have a clear identity. The sense of identity that the phrase 'Temple Bar' evoked was crucial in enlisting the support of seemingly disparate activists.

2 Simplicity and Focus – It is essential that development proposals should be simple and avoid excessive detail. They need to be focused, with clearly stated objectives, and be capable of commanding broad support. It is significant that the Temple Bar Development Council's pro-posals of April 1988 remained unaltered throughout the pre-development phase, and became the basis on which the development proceeded.

3 Consensus – The lessons to be learned from the Temple Bar experience, in translating proposals for development into actual development, revolve largely around effective lobbying, and both identifying and then enlisting the support of those agencies that have the necessary power to achieve specific results. The Temple Bar Development Council's lobbying was particularly effective as its target groups were, fortunately, very receptive to the proposals. Enlisting the support of Dublin Corporation Planning Department and that of the Department of the Taoiseach were the key elements that allowed the development to proceed.

4 Hard Work – Finally, it should be noted that the pre-development phase took three years of hard work by a dedicated body of activists and supporters. We would like to thank all those with whom we had the privilege and pleasure of working during that time.

RICHARD WENTGES is a Dublin-born architect in private practice, who has been living in Temple Bar since 1985. He served as an executive member of the Temple Bar Development Council from 1991-93, and subsequently worked as Community Liaison Officer for Temple Bar Properties Ltd and served as a board member of Temple Bar Renewal Ltd.

JOHN QUILLINAN was the administrator of the Dublin Resource Centre, a workers' co-operative in Crow Street. He was a founder-member of the Temple Bar Development Council in 1988, became its first chairman, and held that position until 1992. He was employed as an executive by Temple Bar Properties Ltd from 1991-96, and is a member of the board of Temple Bar Renewal Ltd.

Dublin Resource Centre, Crow Street

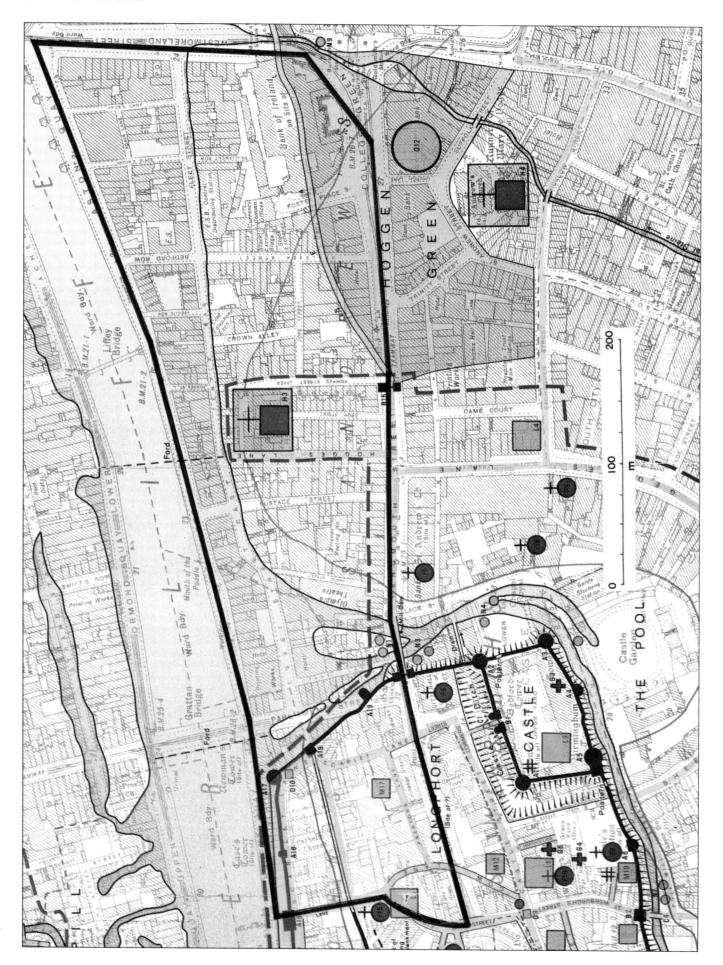

The historical origins of Temple Bar

MARGARET GOWEN

THE REDEVELOPMENT OF TEMPLE BAR AS A CO-ORDINATED EXERCISE HAS PRESENTED both a challenge and an opportunity to study the historical background to the area as a whole, and to evaluate its archaeological potential. The need for archaeological appraisal was identified by Temple Bar Properties at the outset of its work in the locality, and archaeological assessment has formed part of the pre-development (feasibility) study process. This assessment work has served to inform the client, the planning authority, the Office of Public Works and the respective design teams of the nature of the archaeological presence on individual sites, and to identify, for all concerned, the implications for the development of each site in turn. The archaeological study, together with excavation on several sites, has facilitated the preparation of a far more comprehensive picture of the early development of this part of the city than had been previously available.

The archaeological study of Temple Bar is a continuing endeavour. It has kept pace with the redevelopment, and it has also influenced the design of some developments, such as the Essex Quay block where the remains of Isolde's Tower are now displayed. The scale and nature of individual developments tend to dictate the extent to which archaeological study is undertaken, and not all of the sites can be evaluated or studied comprehensively, as the nature of some projects may involve minimal structural intervention.

It is generally accepted that total archaeological excavation of all development sites is neither possible nor desirable. Archaeological excavation is a process of removal (and thereby destruction in its own way), so there is a responsibility to publish the results and make the material available and accessible to the public. It is also widely felt among archaeologists that a percentage of archaeological evidence should

Excavation in progress at Isolde's Tower in Temple Bar

opposite
Temple Bar area superimposed on the medieval town of Dublin, after Clarke (1978)

be left in place for future generations at a time when excavation, survey, conservation and interpretative/display methods may be more sophisticated. The challenge, therefore, is to ensure, by design strategies, that the impact of construction is kept to an absolute minimum, building above the archaeological layers where such an approach is deemed appropriate, while also studying strategically important sites which will inform our present studies of the city.

The two sectors of Temple Bar, east and west, are now divided by Parliament Street, and this topographical divide reflects very different, though related, sequences of archaeological activity.

The archaeology of Temple Bar has been dominated by the River Poddle and its confluence with the Liffey. The Poddle crosses Temple Bar, flowing from Dublin Castle northwards to the Liffey, and originally formed a wide, shallow, fan-shaped estuary which extended from the western side of Parliament Street as far as the back of what is now The Ark on Meeting House Square. The River Liffey shoreline lay some 20-30 metres to the south of Temple Bar / Essex Street East on the east, and followed a line just south of Essex Street West on the west. It was here, on a strategic headland between the two rivers, that the enclosed – and later, walled – Hiberno-Viking and Anglo-Norman town developed.

VIKING PERIOD

At the time of writing, the comprehensive large-scale redevelopment of the area west of Parliament Street has not yet seen its main building phase, but the early phases of development here have led to significant new archaeological discoveries. Excavation beneath The Cutlers at 5-7 Exchange Street / 33-34 Parliament Street yielded radio-carbon dates for very early Viking-period habitation, which may precede the establishment of the main, 10th-century phase of the Viking town for which the excavated evidence is already well established.

The evidence from 33-34 Parliament Street occurred along with evidence for the clay bank enclosures of the early Viking town on the Poddle estuary shoreline. In this location, the series of banks enclosed what became the strategically important northeastern corner of the Viking settlement.

The large vacant site on the south of Essex Street West now holds the key to the interpretation of the early radio-carbon dates, and could possess further new evidence for the earliest Viking settlement of Dublin.

Outside the Viking town and downstream of the Poddle-Liffey confluence, the earliest archaeological activity extended towards Temple Bar from Hoggen Green along Temple Lane (originally Hogges Lane), which is now thought to have possibly formed its western limit. Hoggen Green may have developed around one or more Norse burial mounds, if the Norse word *haugr*, meaning mound, can be considered the derivation of the name. To the west of Hoggen Green, the Thingmount is also thought to have a Norse derivation, and on the basis of recent research, is considered to have been located near South Great George's Street, straddling Dame Street. The Norse word *thing-mot* means a public assembly. Beneath the Green Building at Temple Lane / Crow Street, a small group of Hiberno-Viking pagan burials were revealed beneath burials of the later medieval cemetery (described below).

ANGLO-NORMAN PERIOD

The strategic importance of the northeastern corner of the town on the approach to the city from the river is reflected in the location of Isolde's Tower on the Anglo-Norman city wall. Prior to development at Essex Quay, the presence of the foundations of this tower on the site were suspected, and this was indeed confirmed during pre-planning assessment. The extensive archaeological excavation carried out in the course of the development revealed that Exchange Street Lower derives its particular curvature and configuration from the line of the Anglo-Norman city wall towards Essex Gate. Similarly, it has been established through inspection and pre-development assessment that the particular configuration of the property divisions on the south side of Essex Gate reflect the line of the city wall, which now lies beneath this block. The base of Isolde's Tower, revealed during the excavation, has been preserved, and will be displayed in situ within the development. Also, an innovative engineering scheme has been devised for the Essex Gate site so that the new structure is cantilevered over the remains of the city wall.

At the Viking Adventure site, west of Isolde's Tower, excavation provided evidence for quarrying and an episode of concerted riverfront reclamation during the early 13th century to fill the area between the then defunct Hiberno-Viking wall and the newly built Anglo-Norman wall [Simpson, 1995]. The Viking wall (c.1100) is now thought to lie beneath the Essex Street West frontage, but was not found during the excavation or during exploratory test trenching on the adjacent site to the west.

No Anglo-Norman wooden quayfront development was evident in the excavated area, but a clay bank was constructed as a flood bank during the quarrying phase, behind which reclamation fill was dumped. This clay bank extended westwards, and was discovered in a test trench on the north-east side of Fishamble Street, where it was found to have a planked wooden revetment. Its location can be roughly related to that of the 1210 revetment at Wood Quay.

East of the Poddle and the city, the Augustinian friary of the Holy Trinity was founded around 1257 at the north end of Temple Lane. (Two other ecclesiastical foundations were established at around the same time, located outside the Temple Bar area – one at St Mary de Hogges on the site of St Andrew's Church, and the other at All Hallows on the site of

Trinity College.) The friary cemetery was found on Temple Lane / Crow Street, beneath the Green Building, where 72 burials were excavated and retrieved for study and safe keeping. The supposed location of the friary buildings in the Temple Lane / Cecilia Street / Fownes Street area was not confirmed until very recent archaeological excavation at 5-6 Cecilia Street revealed some of the foundations of friary walls. Here the friary walls were found to have influenced the position of Cecilia Street, which is the only minor street to cross the Essex Street / Dame Street block in an east-west direction, apart from the new Curved Street.

The wide mud-flats of the Poddle estuary were still in existence at the time the friary complex was established. These buildings appear to have been centred on a spit of land bounded by Temple Lane and Fownes Street, which jutted slightly out into the River Liffey at this point. Dame Street is thought to have defined the southern extent of the friary. The estuary still extended as far back as the present-day location of The Ark in Meeting House Square at that time. In this area, one of the shallow channels of the Poddle was diverted into a mill-race (possibly one of several) and used during the early 14th century. The channel silted up rapidly during the later 14th or 15th centuries (dated by pottery in the silt), and was traced during archaeological excavation beneath the Gallery of Photography and along the back of The Ark, out into the river under the National Photographic Archive building. A dendrochronological date of approximately 1345 from a worked timber retrieved from a test trench opened on Meeting House Square may provide evidence for milling, which is likely to have been run by friars.

LATER DEVELOPMENT AND THE QUAYS

The 17th- and 18th-century maps provide much of the evidence for later development in both the eastern and western sectors, and this evidence is often confirmed by the discovery of physical remains, both beneath and within buildings currently being redeveloped or refurbished. The Poddle now runs through a 4m-wide, brick-vaulted culvert, which runs from Dublin Castle, through East Essex Street, where it cuts obliquely through the foundations of Designyard as it heads towards the Liffey. Parts of the culvert were exposed and recorded in the course of the development of Designyard.

The original Liffey shoreline was located well back from its present location, roughly 20m to the south of the present line of Essex Street and Temple Bar. As the eastern area developed during the 16th century, and especially during a surge of development in the mid- and late-17th century, the shoreline was reclaimed with masses of dumped soil, industrial ash and domestic debris, including clay pipes (early forms), wine bottles, old shoes, dumped cobbler's leather, broken pots of all shapes and sizes (including those used in the 'chamber') and food waste, especially animal bones and oyster shells. Examples of all were found during archaeological supervision for the basement of the new Temple Bar Gallery

and Studios, in the adjacent print studios, and in other developments along Wellington Quay. The river was pushed northwards and contained by quay walls, the location of which are represented on John Roque's map of the area. The physical remains of this quay wall eluded discovery until what is thought to be the 17th-century quay wall was located just inside the Wellington Quay side of a site at No.3 Temple Bar.

Further downstream, evidence for the reclamation of the Strand depicted on the de Gomme map of 1673 was revealed during investigation of the Temple Bar Car Park site on Fleet Street. Possible evidence for the location of the original Custom House, also depicted on that map, was seen during a very limited investigation prior to redevelopment of Rumpole's Pub on the east side of Parliament Street, where two phases of demolished red-brick buildings were identified beneath the standing structure. The Wood Yard, also depicted on the map, was found during excavation beneath the National Photographic Archive building on Essex Street East.

Excavations at 5-6 Cecilia Street revealed evidence of the widening of Fownes Street, which was once a simple laneway. Here a buried 17th-century wall ran beneath the present pavement. It formed the east boundary of a property which once lay where the road now runs.

Few of the buildings in Temple Bar have revealed their rich and varied history in quite the same way as the Smock Alley Theatre, at the former church of SS Michael & John on Exchange Street Lower and Essex Street West. In a detailed archaeological and architectural appraisal of the complex, the theatre building was found to be largely intact and to form much of the substance of the later church. Its opes and doorways had been blocked, and later pre-church interventions were evident and were traced and surveyed once the outer plaster had been removed. The foundations of its original front façade and porch were revealed during excavations beneath the church's crypt, and its roof timbers were found – albeit reused – to be those of the earlier building [Simpson, 1996].

The dynamic of redevelopment in the Temple Bar area is the present-day manifestation of an ancient process of selected reuse, new building and integration, dating back to Viking times. It has already been charted in some detail as a result of selected study and excavation to date on the Phase 1 sites (published as a series of reports, 1994-1996), informing and assisting the decision on the appropriate areas of study, and, in particular, excavation to be selected during Phase 2, west of Parliament Street.

MARGARET GOWEN started her professional career in archaeology in 1979, after a year working as a supervisor at the National Museum's Fishamble Street excavations. She has been involved in pre-development archaeological projects and consultancy since then, and now heads a successful professional practice. She was engaged as archaeological consultant to Temple Bar Properties in 1992.

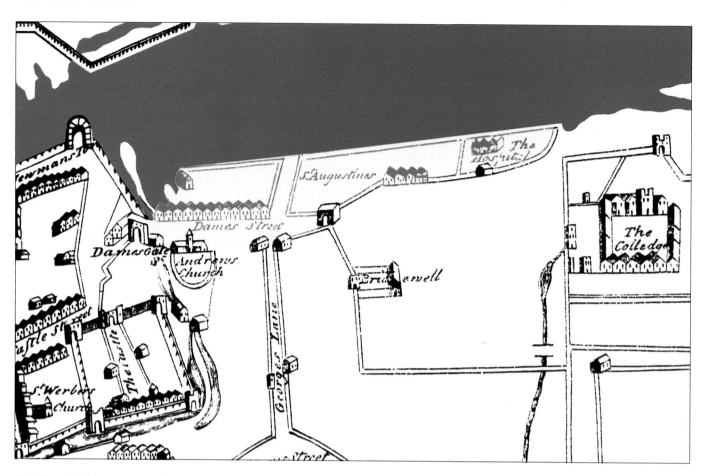

The Temple Bar area superimposed on the Poole & Cash map of 1610 (above), and the John Rocque map of 1757 (below)

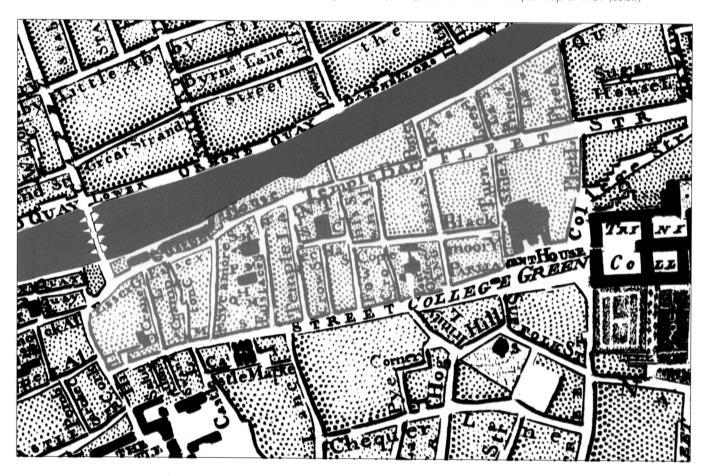

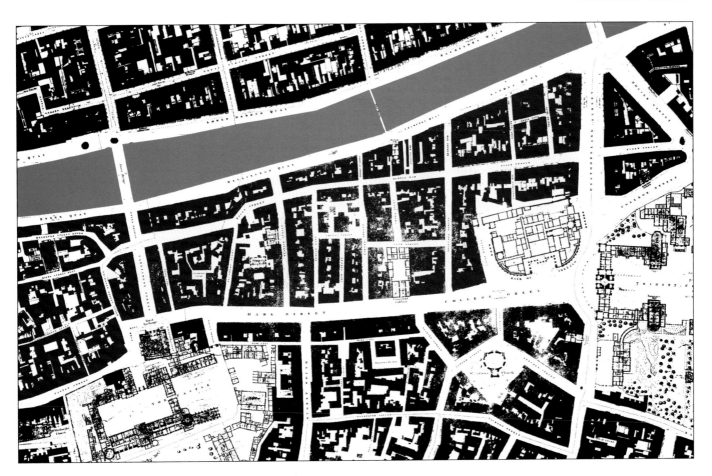

The Temple Bar area superimposed on the Ordnance Survey maps of 1847 (above) and 1987 (below)

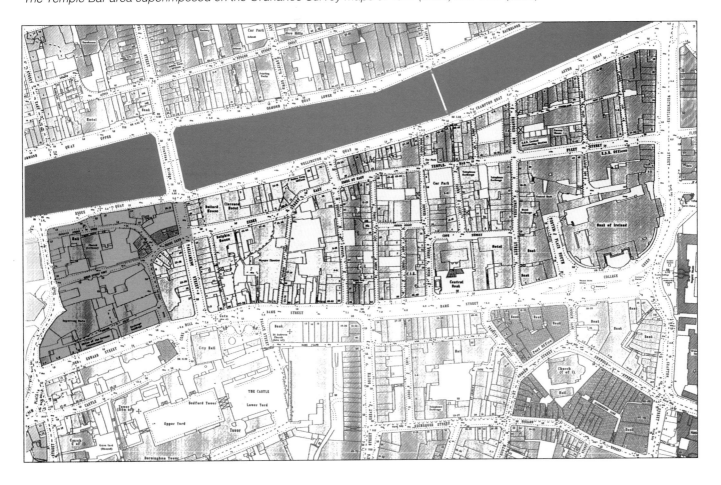

Urban Design

NIALL McCULLOUGH

THE IDEA OF TEMPLE BAR AS A FOCUS FOR URBAN RENEWAL IN Dublin appears inevitable in retrospect only; it is salutary to remember that it might have ended up as a bus station. In fact, the creation of a land bank to implement its destruction allowed for a comprehensive approach to its revitalisation. Today, Temple Bar forms a kind of necessary heart to Dublin which it lacked and which it always needed if the city was to prosper. It has achieved this in physical terms, but also in revising perceptions of Dublin – a city until lately divided into independent mental zones. It has linked up the map in some way. Although it has always been there, it has been invested with some sense of the late 20th-century city, an open, mixed, old/new, ordinary, opportunity-filled place. Significantly, it has been achieved without the destruction of another quarter of the city; it has not replaced anything, but added to the overall.

This sense of the ordinary is important. It is interesting to speculate as to how much the history and particular urban character of the Temple Bar quarter have contributed to its success. It has always had two partly conflicting characteristics: from the Middle Ages it was a well-defined zone, an identifiable parcel of land within the city; and, at the same time, secondary to its main function, a service quarter which was put to wave on wave of use in a complex overlayering of parts – the essence of diverse yet muted normality, which is the engine of city life. Its great period of growth was neither the Middle Ages nor the 18th century, but the period between 1600-1720, a relatively unknown time which defined much of Dublin's structure. It is interesting to remember that these streets were busy with life when Merrion Square and Fitzwilliam Street were still fields.

Its outline can be simply traced in early maps, which appeared, on average, every thirty years through the Classical period. In effect, the rectangle of land was forced by geography to a particular shape by the river to the north and by the dominant east-west axis of Dame Street to the south, linking the oval shape of the medieval city with its ceremonial open space at Hoggen (now College) Green. To the west, it was cut off from the heavily fortified city by the out-

Dame Street, after the Wide Streets Commissioners

flow of the Poddle river, then a widely spreading delta forming part of the city defences. Barely built up (though probably intensely farmed) in the Middle Ages, its major landmark was a little Augustinian monastery (currently under excavation). This was reached from Dame Street via Dirty (Temple) Lane – a medieval route which established the inevitable north-south ladder of streets in the quarter. Temple Bar gained some identity with the establishment of a new custom house and quay in 1620. This development (the building was roughly where Dollard Printers is now) coincided with the canalisation of the edge of the Poddle and a new street to connect the Custom House with Dame Street called Crane Lane, after the city crane which served to unload cargo there. It has some claim to Dublin's first straight Renaissance street. Subsequently, Sycamore Street evolved nearby, its name putatively derived from its relationship with a timber yard beside the water. Following the establishment of the Irish Parliament in Chichester House on College Green, Dame Street began to fill up with the mansions of aristocratic landowners, who laid out pleasure gardens behind, leading to the Liffey. This world of Caroline Dublin society has completely vanished from public perception. Its achievements faded in the twenty years of warfare that followed 1641.

As with so much else in Dublin, the arrival of the Duke of Ormonde as Viceroy in 1660 galvanised the city as the capital of Ireland. In Temple Bar, it coincided with the extension of the quay wall along the Liffey, and a new street backfilled alongside – Fleet Street, Temple Bar, Essex Street. This confirmed the quarter's potential – no longer a series of gardens and dead ends, but a 'serviced' zone ripe for construction. Patterns of development were typical of the time. Families who owned land prepared it by providing a skeleton of streets (maximising land use) and offered plots to lease for a number of years. These were taken and built up by individuals and groups, ensuring a diversity of building types and sizes within an overall framework. The urban designs prepared on each piece of land were 'Classical' in intent, but as

the holdings were small and set cheek-by-jowl with similar holdings, the overall plan of the city has a kind of disjointed and conditional pattern – an assembly of ordered fragments which becomes completely logical and comprehensible once the background is understood.

Temple Bar was laid out in two waves: Essex Street and Essex Bridge were established in the 1670s; Eustace Street (built on the garden of the Eustace family mansion) dates from the 1680s; Anglesea Street from some years later. The quays were Corporation property, and leased by them to provide Aston Quay. On Temple Bar itself, the houses (including several famous brothels) backed directly on to the water, the inhabitants taking tea next to the rigging of the seagoing ships which had to unload there. Later, the sequence of Crow Street, Cecilia Street, Cope Street and Fownes Street were added, and are visible in Brooking's Map of 1728. The western end was already built up as part of the medieval city.

During this time, Temple Bar was the heart of the city, set between two great foci – the Custom House on Essex Quay (grandly rebuilt in 1707, its façade traditionally lit by thousands of candles to celebrate King George's birthday) and the Theatre Royal in Crow Street. Before the mid-century, the streets around already boasted as many banks, taverns and Dissenter meeting houses as houses. Late 18th-century Georgian Dublin grew up around Temple Bar and redefined its edges in an almost over-emphatic manner. The Wide Streets Commissioners, whose mission empowered them to create new and generous streets through the existing fabric of the city, created Parliament Street (1757) to link Essex Bridge and Dublin Castle. The uniform shops and houses remain in outline towering over Crane Lane. Dame Street was comprehensively widened in sections over a ninety-year period (the buildings on Dame Street between Temple Lane and Crow Street are Wide Streets Commissioners' work of the 1840s). In the 1790s Westmoreland Street was driven from College Green to Carlisle (O'Connell) Bridge. Finally, in a

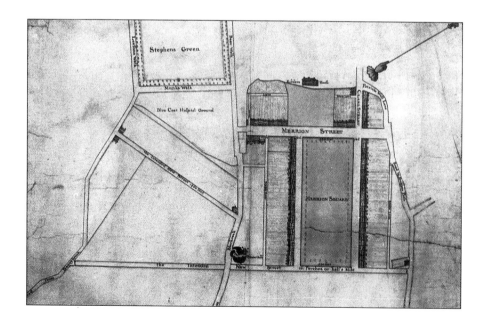

James Ensor's 1762 plan for Merrion Square

grand plan to link the quays into a continuous thoroughfare on both banks (they were originally conceived as individual terraces over water), Wellington Quay was extended from Aston Quay to Parliament Street. Wide Streets Commissioners' houses and shopfronts survive here as well. The new quay was so close to pre-existing Temple Bar that several buildings are extremely thin and closely built back to back. The Victorian impact was relatively light – offices, warehouses and factories set into the narrow streets, completing a dense and varied range of building types, from possibly 17th-century houses to early 18th-century Dutch Billies, like 25 Eustace Street, Georgian houses, warehouses and shops – a heritage left to gradually fall apart in the modern era.

The comprehensive revitalisation in Temple Bar depended absolutely on these realities established over time – mixed buildings providing large, open rooms and small, intimate, panelled spaces, the grid of north-south streets with unusually close back-to-back dimensions, often infilled and built over, the subtle hierarchy of use from east to west, the clear edges creating an identity, and the empty sites and gaps left between buildings, offering opportunity for infill development. In many ways, although precedents do exist elsewhere, all necessary precedent for a complex and sophisticated renewal lay within the area itself, in its overlayering of Renaissance on medieval, the intrusion of the Wide Streets Commissioners, the humane scale of Victorian modernity. This work could only have happened in this way in Temple Bar, and was most successful because of it.

Precedent does exist elsewhere, both for the character of the area and for the theme of intervention to create change; seldom, however, for both together. Soho in London has been a kind of unspoken parallel, the Marais in Paris, the Jordaan in Amsterdam, all, interestingly, dated for the same 17th-century period which perhaps allowed sufficient time for a decline and an overlayering not available to younger quarters. Precedent for comprehensive intervention – usually based on

low-cost housing – is familiar. It even existed in the Guinness estate and the Liberties of Dublin, where major intervention works to stabilise and enhance decaying urban areas took place. It has also been a theme of later 20th-century attitudes to city renewal – in Paris and in the IBA of Berlin in the 1980s, where dozens of low-cost housing schemes were introduced with varying architectural and social success into the fabric of the broken city.

In many ways, the closest equivalent to Dublin's use of cultural buildings to lead change is Frankfurt-am-Main, where the image of a dull financial centre was transformed by the building of world-class museums by well-known architects around the city. In Temple Bar, new cultural (and commercial) buildings as small-scale urban interventions have been successful in themselves and as urban design tools, delivering a greatly articulated and logical sequence of movement via public spaces across the area. The interior of blocks have been taken on and opened up. Although it could so easily have been done badly, the location of these interventions are almost self-evident, given the particularly conducive environment. Although the cultural aspect of development has been important, it is in some ways not critical to the area's success, which is founded more on the recreation of urban possibility, on the idea of not only living in the city, but living well in the city, of a city which has changed, but is alive and may change again, which involves the intelligent reuse of ordinary buildings without 'themed' façades, and contains the seeds of its own regeneration. That will be the real legacy of Temple Bar in Dublin, and perhaps in the wider contexts as well.

NIALL McCULLOUGH is a partner in McCullough Mulvin Architects, Dublin, and a member of Group 91, a consortium of practices which won the Temple Bar Framework Plan competition. He has written several books, including *Dublin: An Urban History*, on the evolution of the city.

Late 18th-century urban interventions by the Wide Streets Commissioners

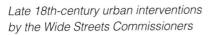

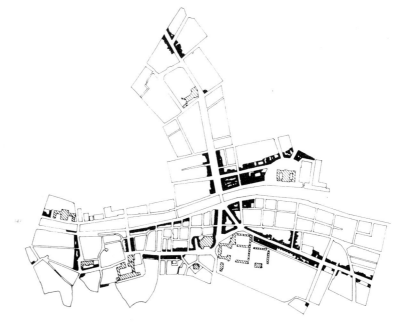

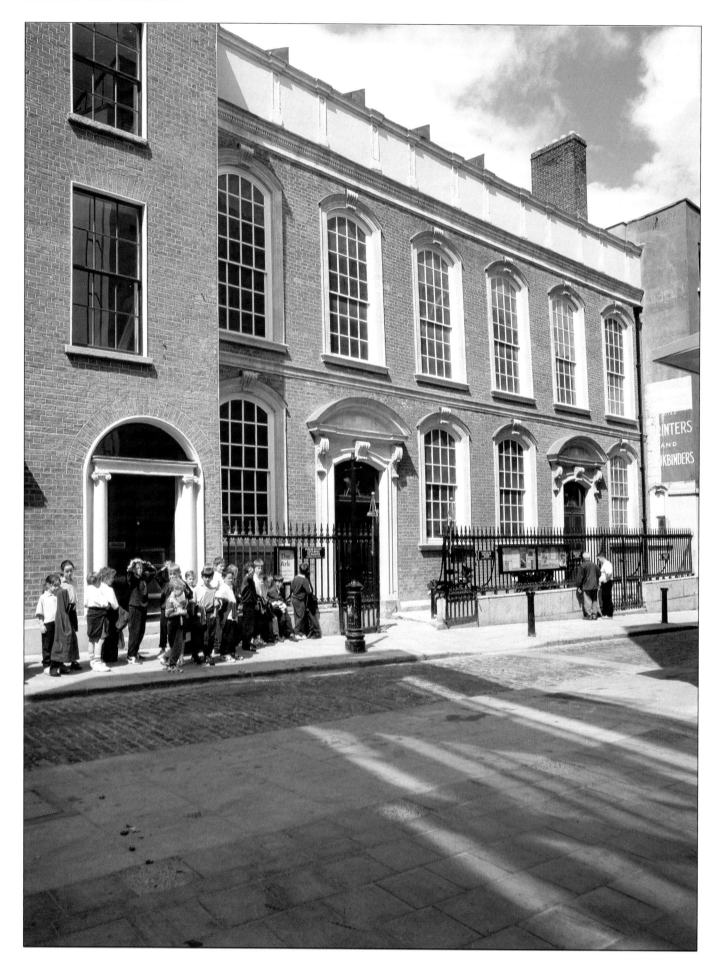

The rôle of the architectural inventory in urban revitalisation

LOUGHLIN KEALY

REVITALISING URBAN AREAS MEANS ENSURING CONTINUITY AND GENERATING CHANGE. The need for continuity and change applies to both the physical fabric of streets and buildings and to the social fabric made up by the people who live and work in them. Today's conception of the 'living city' has acquired fresh nuances of meaning: the city is seen as shaping the life experience, the thoughts, the memory and the imagination of its inhabitants. Increasingly, it is the factor of human consciousness, and the place of the built environment within it, that is the focus of critical attention in the closing years of this century. In a world of images and shifting realities, the physical fabric of the city is a positive anchor in space and time, helping to ground the identity of its inhabitants. Yet, like any living system, the city changes to survive, and how well it does so depends largely on how well it learns from experience.

Dublin is a city in the process of transforming its physical environment. The re-building of the quays and the creation of the cultural quarter in Temple Bar are well advanced; the rejuvenation of Smithfield and the redevelopment of the Docklands are major undertakings; the transportation projects will revolutionise the relationship of the city centre to the suburbs. The Temple Bar experiment has been intense and, within the lifetime of the city of Dublin, very short. Because of its very intensity and brevity, it provides an opportunity to see how the relationship of continuity and change has been managed, and perhaps to learn some lessons from the experience. This essay looks at one aspect of a complex and exciting experience: the gathering of information about existing buildings through an architectural inventory, and the how this fitted in to the wider picture.

The former Presbyterian Meeting House on Eustace Street (1725), now The Ark, a children's cultural centre (Group 91 / Shane O'Toole and Michael Kelly Architects)

As far as the built environment in concerned, managing continuity and change involves a broad spectrum of possible intervention, ranging from complete preservation at one end of the scale to new building at the other. The architectural inventory is an essential tool for doing this well. Given that alteration of existing buildings and the replacement of old buildings with new ones are part of the process of urban evolution, the most immediate application of the inventory is in identifying buildings and urban settings of special value, so that they are either exempted from that process, or so that the impact of change can be modified to protect those things that are considered important. The twin aims in building conservation are to avoid loss of material resource and cultural value, while making older buildings suitable for contemporary living. If the process of identification is haphazard or selective, or if the criteria used for designating buildings and urban landscapes to be protected are not transparent, this will prove to be an impossible task.

THE CITY AND THE ARCHITECTURAL INVENTORY

Existing street and plot patterns are important measures of urban scale, as well as being the armature for the architecture of the city. Buildings accommodate the living functions of the city, are important expressions of its cultural aspirations over time, and constitute a major material and economic resource. Thus the operating brief for the architectural inventory requires that streets and buildings should be recorded in ways that facilitate good decision-making in architecture, urban design and planning. Effective management demands good information. As far as the built environment is concerned, this means information that describes fully what exists, places the existing in the context of its past, and provides for future possibilities according to the values placed on these two. Such information is an essential foundation for the preparation of framework plans. Allowing at this stage for the begged questions, one can say that information needs to be comprehensive and accurate and the judgements of value need to be soundly based in a process that invites consensus.

Generally speaking, in this country we have little experience of creating architectural inventories, and even less experience of dealing with the kind of information that a comprehensive architectural inventory provides. It is only in the past few years that systematic attempts have been made to record the architectural heritage. The National Architectural Inventory being conducted by the Office of Public Works has recorded a number of Irish towns, including major centres such as Carlow, Clonmel, Dundalk and Kilkenny. Dublin has not been included up to now in the OPW survey. However, the Dublin Environmental Inventory (DEI), which was a pilot project funded by the European Commission under the LIFE programme in 1993, developed a systematic approach to recording streets and buildings, and has covered many important buildings in the city. Developed by a project team in the School of Architecture, UCD, the approach was mod-

elled on the National Inventory, but was customised for the special requirements of the capital. In 1994, this project team was asked by Temple Bar Properties to carry out a similar architectural inventory for the Temple Bar area, using the DEI system.

Returning to the broader picture for the moment, one notes that other organisations, such as the Irish Architectural Archive, An Taisce and more recently, the Civic Trust, have compiled information on the built environment of Dublin, each working to its own methods. These various inventories need to be brought together, and the information in them vetted through a consistent validation process, if we are ever to have the kind of comprehensive information needed to manage the physical environment of the city.

THE TEMPLE BAR ARCHITECTURAL INVENTORY

Survey work for the Temple Bar inventory began in June and ended in December 1995. As with the Dublin i0nventory, there were two kinds of record created, a visual record and a documentary record.
• The visual record is mainly photographic, and consists of high-grade photographs of the principal elevation of buildings. The intention was to assemble these together to give a composite picture of each side of a street, but the narrowness of some streets and lanes occasionally required adjustments to be made. In addition, typical views of each street are recorded. Survey drawings of selected buildings form a secondary part of the visual record.
• The documentary record consists of a written description of each street and building, recording what was there at the time the inventory was carried out, and also detailing the history of the streets and buildings from a wide range of historical sources. There are numerous headings or categories in these descriptions so that the information can be very detailed. Since the system is designed to be flexible, all the information has been entered on computer, so that it can be corrected if errors are discovered and up-dated as new developments take place.

The work on the Temple Bar inventory was of considerable benefit to the ongoing task of developing the overall DEI system. Concentrating on a compact area like Temple Bar meant that aspects of the overall approach could be tested more quickly, and as a result the DEI system was modified and improved. The major impact was to confirm the usefulness of dealing with streets as a whole as well as documenting individual buildings. At the time of writing, the Temple Bar inventory is not yet complete. While the fieldwork for the first phase was being carried out, a great deal of construction was underway throughout the area. Since several of the key projects, and important elements such as the two new squares, were not yet finished, it was recognised that the inventory would need to be updated in due course. There are also some gaps in the information that could be gathered in the allotted time – for a variety of reasons it was not always possible to gain access to buildings when the fieldwork was underway, so there is a need to supplement the information provided in the data base. Despite this, the inventory provides a resource which, if it is maintained, will prove invaluable with the passage of time.

The Temple Bar inventory was carried out when the implementation of the framework plan was already underway, and so was not available as an input to the decision-making process. One of the principal benefits of a comprehensive inventory is that it allows one to identify buildings that should be kept at all costs, those that can be modified to one degree or another, and those of little architectural, historical or urban landscape interest. It is difficult to say with confidence that, had a complete inventory been available, controversial decisions affecting notable existing buildings would not have been made. Would such an inventory have made a difference in respect to the unlisted houses on Essex Quay, whose demolition was to reveal the remains of medieval fortifications? Would it have helped illuminate the importance of the former Church of SS Michael & John? There is no doubt that many of Dublin's older buildings incorporate significant remains of earlier structures, a point underlined by the discovery, through archaeological investigation of the church, of surviving fabric of Smock Alley Theatre.

A comprehensive architectural inventory cannot guarantee that all surviving fabric will be discovered. Very often it does indicate where in-depth examination is needed. Nor can the inventory guarantee that, if the full facts are established, correct decisions will be made. Occasionally, conflicting priorities will emerge with regard to heritage issues, and we have yet to develop satisfactory methods of resolving conflicting cultural values. The overriding issue as far as the Temple Bar area is concerned is, rather, that the inventory was not seen as an essential requirement in developing the framework plan. This is a key issue with implications beyond the boundaries of Temple Bar.

Most of the systematic gathering of information on the buildings of Dublin has been carried out by non-statutory bodies. In the meantime, both the local authorities and the private sector operate with piecemeal information for which there is no uniform system of validation. There is widespread agreement about the need for reliable data, but in the dynamics of urban regeneration, in the day-to-day pressures of planning and development control, generating such data can be seen as a costly and time-consuming exercise. The fact that so many diverse sources of information on the built heritage of the city exist side by side shows that the need for a comprehensive inventory is not understood at the appropriate levels; far less is the potential of the inventory envisaged. Intervention is needed at government level to develop, expand and accelerate the process of recording the built environment in an integrated fashion. Otherwise progress will be too slow, and inventories will continue to be seen as luxuries rather than as essential and dynamic instruments of environmental policy.

© Dublin Environmental Inventory Ltd   School of Architecture University College Dublin

Street Inventory Form

Street Name	Fownes Street
Previous Address	Fownes Street Lower was originally known as Bagnio Slip in the 16th Century.
Number on Plan	K28
Plan and Quadrant	DEI DCSE
Sector and Block	Sector f: Blocks 31k/32k
O.S. Map Number	3263/10

Current Description

Fownes Street runs north-south between Wellington Quay and Dame Street and is separated into upper and lower streets. Fownes Street Lower runs for 30m from Wellington Quay to its intersection with Temple Bar. It is 7m wide with pavements on both sides carrying one-way traffic from Temple Bar to Wellington Quay. Fownes Street Upper is split into two parts by a pedestrian area between Cecilia Street and Cope Street. From Cope Street, Fownes Street Upper runs for 70m turning into Dame Street. From Temple Bar, Fownes Street Upper runs south for 60m sloping up and turning west into Cecilia Street.

Laid out as part of the post-1650s development of Temple Bar Fownes Street - despite recent losses - remains a local street in the district. At the south end its west range retains a series of early eighteenth century houses unique in Ireland, of small scale and low rise but with broad plots. With the loss of the east range due to the development of the Central Bank, these houses now open to the grandiose modern scale of the Bank's plaza. The lower sections of the street retain little evidence of their origins, with extensive alterations and additions and numerous losses.

The east side of Fownes Street Lower is formed by a single block of buildings three storey with the corner to Temple Bar being a vacant site and used as a car park. The gable end of no.2 faces onto this area and is painted with a mural. The west side is made by the side elevation of no.41 Wellington Quay and one elevation of Temple Bar Gallery and Studios. The street is cobbled along the roadway with granite pavements on either side. All buildings are directly to the street and the pavement to the new gallery is embedded with lights sequenced to direct to the main entrance on Temple Bar. There is no parking on this section of the street and the roadway is most often used by pedestrians as the pavements are quite narrow.

Fownes Street Upper is split into a further two sections. From Temple Bar the east side of the street will be formed by the soon to be completed Temple Bar Square. This is followed by a three storey six building block of varying facade type with a stepped street and parapet line. The west side from Temple Bar is a single block with an arched opening allowing vehicle access to a small courtyard midway along the street; the remainder is an open site used as a car park enclosed by a head height brick wall. The roadway is again fully cobbled with concrete and granite pavements. The street and the roadway vary in width according to the facade line.

The roadway from Fownes Street turns west into Cecilia Street while the east facade and pavement continues becoming a pedestrian area the width of the street and meets with Cope Street. The west facade is reinstated with a newly completed apartment building turning the corner from Cecilia Street. This block runs to Dame street as the remaining west side to Fownes Street Upper and is made by a variety of building facade types; notable ones being numbers 3 to 6 which are some of the earliest Georgian houses in the city and currently undergoing refurbishment. Also of note is number 1 'The Foggy Dew'; a late Victorian public house. This section of roadway is also cobbled with narrow pavements to both sides. The street is lit by facade mounted iron lamps. Traffic is one-way from Cope Street to Dame Street.

The east side of Fownes Street from Cope Street to Dame street is given over to the site line of the Central Bank. To the street there is a low plinth wall with planters behind with a step access to the open plaza facing Dame Street. The scale of the Central Bank is such that its inhabited floors begin at the parapet level of the surrounding buildings. Fownes Street therefore has no real street edge along this side. The structural block of the bank is so far recessed as to be separated form the street entirely. Consequently the street loses any sense of containment and direction. The domination of the Central Bank gives Fownes Street Upper a distinct character as the complete west street facade is clearly visible to be read as a whole. From Dame Street to Cope Street; Fownes Street on one side the east side having been replaced by the Central Bank. The result is that the west facade of the street has something of the quality of a stage set.

Importance National. Strong urban character and important buildings.

K28.1

Context

Fownes Street Upper and Lower cuts a central route through the core of Temple Bar. The district at present defined as Temple Bar is located in the centre of Dublin on the south side of the Liffey and is bounded by the river Liffey; Fishamble Street; Dame Street and Westmorland Street. Temple Bar takes its name from William Temple - a fellow of King's College Cambridge and a Provost of Trinity in the early seventeenth century - part of whose mansion and gardens is incorporated in the area. The district - originally extending east from the medieval city walls west of Parliament Street towards the river - was laid out on rectilinear street plan from c.1658. This gained it the distinction of being one of the earliest post-medieval developments outside the walls of Dublin castle. After the building of Thomas Burgh's new Custom House in 1707 - along what is now Wellington Quay - the main access was from Temple Bar - giving a new impetus to its commercial development. The small scale of streets and narrow plots largely survived the extensive developments of the capital from the eighteenth century - a procedure distinguished notably by the work of the Wide Streets Commission. The Commission's streets of Dame Street, Parliament Street and Westmorland Street cut around the borders of the original Temple Bar, allowing it to maintain a discreet integrity. Through its historic location between the medieval Castle and the Renaissance Parliament House it has also gained a unique significance. Its survival is also due to an aborted development policy by CIE - a national transport body - which bought property in the area and - letting it out at temporary and economic rates - discouraged more modern development.

Listed Buildings

List 2; No.s 1; 2-5; 5a

Monuments	Features
Bronze seat with engraving on stone base at junction with Cecilia Street.	Stone sets to be retained under List 5 (whole of Fownes Street Lower and part of Fownes Street Upper) Features under List 6

Form Storage	Recorder
School of Architecture UCD	Ciaran O'Brien

Historical Account

The streets name derives from from Sir William Fownes; Sheriff of Dublin 1697 and elected Lord Mayor in 1708. Before it was developed Fownes Street Lower was known as Bagnio Slip where a ferry station was positioned at the slipway. Originally the street was residential but because of proximity to the financial institutions of Dame Street and College Street it became more commercially oriented. From the nineteenth century the unpretentious scale of the houses left them less touched by developers, though they did fall into varying degrees of disrepair and are only now being restored - at least in part. The East side of the street at the upper end was demolished in the 1970s in preparation for the building of the Central Bank.

In 1846 No. 19 was the office of Thomas Reynolds; Marshal of Dublin and Registrar of Pawnbrokers in Ireland. Arthur Griffith (founder of Sinn Fein) had his office in Fownes Street from where he issued "The United Irishman"; (John Temple once owned the same building). The tavern the Golden Cup was here (Thomas Moyies; An 18th century Miscellany; DHR; June-Aug 1948; p.50.). John Angell(?) Prof. of Stenography lived at No. 7 in 1781 (DHR; Vol.XIII; 1953; p.108).

Photographic Context	Cartographic Record
Photographs from both ends of the street plus additional shots from points along street in both directions Photographer Ciaran O'Brien Kr05n01/6.10.94c; Kr05n02/6.10.94c Kr05n03/6.10.94c; Kr05n04/6.10.94c Kr05n09/6.10.94c; Kr05n10/6.10.94c	Rocque 1756 Scale 1773 Poole and Cash 1780 Faden 1797 Taylor 1816

THE ARCHITECTURAL INVENTORY AND ITS WIDER USES

Apart from its primary functions of identifying and recording buildings and areas of value, there are three key applications of architectural inventories which illustrate their importance in the process of urban revitalisation: their role in urban design, their role with regard to new uses for historic buildings, and their contribution to the question of new architecture in historic settings.

1 – The Urban Context

Properly structured and regulated as part of the planning permission process, the architectural inventory is a base for urban design. Both the Dublin Environmental Inventory and the Temple Bar inventory provide detailed information on the urban spaces in which the buildings are set, as well as documenting the buildings themselves. That information is essential because the streets and squares are primary urban elements, and if the data base focused primarily on their constituent buildings, it would be difficult to give sufficient weight to the ensemble.

Architectural distinction and historical significance are not the only criteria for conservation. Urban areas are deemed worthy of protection by virtue of their contribution to contemporary culture, and through acquiring cultural significance with the passage of time – a fact recognised by the international charters on the protection of historic towns and urban districts.

The visual record of buildings and streets can also be used to assess the compatibility of proposed new buildings with the existing setting. It can be used to generate guidelines on building heights, as well as providing a means of evaluating the visual impact of the new building. Historic plot widths can be used to establish an armature for the planning and articulation of new development. These applications are already part of established urban design practice elsewhere. They will, no doubt, find their way into common practice here also.

2 – New Uses for Old Buildings

Where the aim is to avoid unnecessary material and cultural waste, the primary guide to new uses for old buildings lies in the characteristics of the buildings themselves – their form, construction, load-bearing capacity of the floors, and so on. Unless an informed assessment of these characteristics has been made, the likelihood is that the interior will be destroyed in the attempt to make the building suitable for a whole range of new uses. Floors will be expected to carry loadings beyond the capacity of the existing construction. An additional factor is the application of the current Building Regulations, which can require traditional construction to perform to a standard equivalent to that of modern construction. One can argue for greater flexibility in interpreting the Regulations, but it has to be said that it is unreasonable to demand flexibility from individuals when the underlying principle of equivalence is at fault.

There are professional judgements involved, and questions of attitude and knowledge as well. The critical balance between retaining existing fabric and creative re-use of a building is distorted by the lack of good records of what exists and of informed assessment of its value. Unfortunately, 'refurbishment' has too often come to mean skips over-flowing with the debris of gutted interiors, where experience suggests that, if there were sufficient will, the existing construction and detail could be retained and the building returned to effective use. To say this is not to argue for the unthinking preservation of every old building, but it is to say that certain existing buildings are assets that should not be squandered and that the architectural inventory is a vehicle through which the value of the building can be established.

Photogrammetric survey of Fownes Street from the Temple Bar Architectural Inventory

previous page
Sample pages on Fownes Street from the Temple Bar Architectural Inventory

Once the essential information is recorded, architectural inventories can be structured to provide a basis for deciding what new uses should be permitted. As precedent, there is the example of the city of Bologna, where the architectural inventory led to a three-step process: the identification of the various types of historical building; the establishment of a range of allowable uses for each building type; and the definition of how conservation and renovation should be approached for each type, formalised in technical guidelines and regulations.[1]

3 – New Buildings in Historic Settings

Knowledge of urban and building typologies provides the key to both the skilful and imaginative transformation of existing buildings and the creation of new architecture, and the architectural inventory is an important vehicle in creating that knowledge. The international charters, which set down principles for the protection of historic buildings and urban areas, also oppose the artificial freezing of historic areas, recognise the contribution of new architecture to urban revitalisation, and call for the integration of historic areas into the mainstream of contemporary life.[2] Part of that integration will inevitably involve the replacement of unfit fabric and the creation of new buildings.

It is widely recognised that the Temple Bar experiment has been midwife to some of the best of contemporary Irish architecture. Among the designers responsible for this work are architects who have, over the years, explored the relationship of new architecture to inherited building types and urban contexts. The production of new buildings in historic settings, the reuse of historic buildings and their conservation, are interrelated elements of the contemporary architectural challenge, although they sometimes appear to be in opposition. But particular knowledge and skill are required. Architects need to know buildings deeply, and to know about the kind of architecture that creatively retains and transforms rather than destroys. The architectural inventory provides a baseline and essential point of departure.

IN CONCLUSION

As in other fields, there is a kind of critical mass involved in creating a situation in which architectural inventories can exercise the kind of influence described. Ultimately it comes down to whether we can learn from experience. The experiments to date, including that of the Temple Bar inventory, suggest that, at the technical level at least, it can be done, and that the baseline for monitoring change can be established. The architectural inventory is not a panacea for effective management of the built environment, but it is a technical device through which the urban context can find its value in planning and urban design.

Footnotes

[1] Bandarin, Francesco, 'The Bologna Experience: Planning and Historic Renovation in a Communist City' in *The Conservation of European Cities*, Appleyard, D (ed.) (MIT Press, London, 1979)
[2] ICOMOS, *Charter for the Protection of Historic Towns and Districts*, Washington 1987, and the Council of Europe, *Convention for the Protection of the Architectural Heritage of Europe* (Granada, 1985)

LOUGHLIN KEALY is a lecturer in the School of Architecture, University College Dublin, and Director of postgraduate studies in Urban and Building Conservation. He was Director of the Survey of the Built Environment, Dublin Environmental Inventory, and of the Temple Bar Architectural Inventory. He is a member of the Standing Committee on Architecture of the Heritage Council, and the Irish Committee of ICOMOS.

Let's take another look at where we live

DAVID MACKAY

'**W**HAT LOOKS THE STRONGEST HAS OUTLIVED ITS TERMS. THE FUTURE LIES WITH what's affirmed from under.' This quote from Seamus Heaney puts us on guard against both fixed and current ideas, and points, like Darwin, to the emerging, doubtful and insecure ideas that one finds occurring from all different corners of the city.

One of the most important developments in architectural thought in Europe at this moment is the value of recognising problems detected elsewhere, and their solutions, and having the ability of not just transferring them geographically from one country to another, but translating them into the context of a different culture.

Let's take a few examples to explain this. If one stays in any one of an international chain of hotels, one may have the comfort of a familiar interior but be unsure of which city one is staying in. Even the menu could be the same. Or one finds different competing cities collecting works by well-known architects and wanting a fashionable image of a white museum or the latest decorative high-tech device that could be anywhere. These are examples of transferring architecture from one place to another.

Translating architecture is a much more demanding task. An example of this can be found in the pioneer work of the Hertfordshire schools in England and similar work in Denmark in the fifties, based on some experimental schools before the 1939-45 war. Recognising the social content of education, spaces used only for circulation

Mixed-use development of apartments and retail units at Temple Bar Square (Group 91 / Grafton Architects)

*opposite
The raised courtyard of the Printworks at East Essex Street (Group 91 / Derek Tynan Architects)*

were incorporated into extended teaching and learning areas. In other words, single-function spaces became multi-functional. Depending on the cultural and social attitudes of each country or region, this revolutionary typology for educational spaces could be translated into the vocabulary of each specific place. This concerns function, but it is also true of form. For example, the Arts and Crafts movement at the turn of the century in England developed an awareness of traditional means of construction, together with a certain expression of modernity, with the introduction of horizontal strips of windows under the eaves of the roof and corner windows. This was vigorously translated into what is now known as the Amsterdam School. Of course, things are a little more complex, because we can trace the horizontal influence of the American architect Frank Lloyd Wright and also the vertical elegance of the late Viennese Secession.

The immediate post-war years witnessed an almost frenetic attempt to build a brave new world in nearly every European city. The radical ideas of functional clarity, open space and a rational approach to transport inspired most of the town-planners and architects during the fifties. The need for a massive effort to provide new housing led to a rational industrialisation of the means and methods of construction, where economy and quantity were paramount objectives of both the public and private sectors of the building industry. This led to an excessive use of the so-called building 'block' – simple to design, simple to build – and single-function buildings – buildings for living, buildings for working, buildings for shopping – which, in turn, lead to the fragmentation of the city itself – shopping areas, business districts and endless fields of housing blocks. The size of these new housing containers, either long and large or tall and distant, erupted within the historic city and town centres, providing a startling contrast in scale with whatever was left of the existing urban structure.

About thirty years ago I had the opportunity to accompany the architectural critic and historian Sibyl Moholy-Nagy – the widow of the Bauhaus teacher Laszlo – around Barcelona. Looking at a recently built building, she made a remark that has remained with me as a revelation of how to criticise constructively any building of whatever epoch. She waved her hand around in circles, as if cleaning a window, and said, 'It is all quite easy for architects to design the middle of their buildings, but it is the edge that counts, how the building turns a corner, meets the ground and the sky.' A few years later, Louis Kahn, also on a visit to Barcelona, told me something similar: 'It's the joints that count, where one material meets another.'

Edges, or frontiers, are obviously emotional stimulants, when the land finishes and the sea begins, when we cross the controls between one culture and another, when a door opens and we are invited inside. Architecture has a lot to do with edges, and it is one of these that has recently attracted a revived interest amongst many European cities concerned about the progressive degrading aspects of their home town. It is the edge between architecture and town planning, an edge between professions. In Dublin, Temple Bar has been to the forefront of this emerging future 'from under'.

For too long there has been no link between architecture and town planning. Each has been going its own way – Moholy-Nagy's middle piece – leaving the design of the public space, the urban room, the character of a street, to the wilderness of chance. Contrary to popular opinion, the design of our villages, towns and cities has always been a result of careful thought, either through the slow traditions established by the weather, safety and trade routes, or through reasons of military defence and the hierarchy of power, be it civil or religious. With the fast expansion of urban life – due to the industrial revolution – these traditions were rapidly eroded and the unhealthy and socially deprived conditions of many urban areas were met with the rational challenge of a functional city – the Charter of Athens in 1933 – which formed the basis of all post-war reconstruction in the definition of the city's four functions: housing, work, recreation (during leisure) and traffic. Planning was to determine the structure of each of these sectors assigned to the four key functions, and would fix their respective locations within the whole. From Stockholm to Rome and from Glasgow to Moscow, the functional city sowed the seeds of social division, despair and loss of identity. The real function of the city had been forgotten. Another look was necessary.

By political accident – tragic in many ways – Spanish cities were isolated by the Franco dictatorship and its limited economy from this functional rebuilding of its city centres. This meant that professional architects and town-planners not involved with the Franco regime were, within the academic precincts of the university, able to establish a critical approach to the reconstruction of our towns and cities. Rather than establishing a new theory of urban design, it is perhaps more accurate to define this approach to considerations of an empirical nature, a more profound awareness of the reality of what the city has meant to our society, economy and culture, and what it can offer as a necessary part of modern-day life. With the dawn of a new democracy, Spanish cities, and Barcelona in particular, have had the opportunity to benefit from the close understanding by both politicians and the professions of the necessity to establish a new and fresh approach to the problems of urban design. This, it must be admitted, was also in response to a strong grass-roots neighbourhood demand for a more decent and socially responsive urban environment. The public was claiming its right to determine the public space of its city and no longer leave it as the left-over bits of development. Needless to say, once the standards were set – with built examples of renovated public space – by the public sector, the private developers were generally quick to respond to the increased value of the adjoining property with higher standards of quality.

What are these emerging considerations on the criteria and instruments of urban development in the expansion and reconstruction of a city? And can they be translated into other cultural contexts, and not just transferred?

FORM AND USE

The first thing is to understand that the city is an efficient provider of information and allows many options for social contacts, and physical access to many different places, and, as such, it is a necessary part of modern-day life. The capacity to provide information in these conurbations is exceptional in its wealth and complexity, seldom found in other places or in other circumstances. In the city are gathered together not only the great centres of promotion and production – industry, commerce, finance, arts, teaching, leisure, sport, etc – but also a density and active disorder that are characteristic of the city itself and have important further consequences: citizens easily find out what they want to know about, but they also get information that they were not seeking specifically and which, in principle, they were not interested in. The life of the inhabitants is changing in unpredictable ways and is enriched by both sought-after and chance information. Moreover, the city provides another kind of typically modern convenience: fast access for its inhabitants to the things they have found out about, an access and adaptation made possible through basic features of the city, its level of social integration and physical proximity.

In the modern city, we have to accept a certain tendency towards disorder, necessary for it to achieve its aims, to provide information and access within its own barely systematic confines. For this reason, old ideas about urban zoning and criteria for classifying the functional city are mistaken. We must go back to thinking of the city as a point where functions are superimposed, not just because of the continuity of the urban environment and physical and social associations, but also because of its efficiency in the provision of information and access. On the other hand, in order for this instrument of information and access to be useful to the inhabitants, the formal expression of its contents must be readily intelligible. Therefore, we should acknowledge the fundamental importance of the shape the city takes. Only with a suitable reading of the city can maximum performance in terms of information and access be achieved. To do this, the communicative power of traditional formal elements must be harnessed: streets, avenues, squares, gardens, monuments, architectural façades, etc. Although these elements may have undergone great changes over the years, they have always maintained a clear structure, probably because they have deep anthropological roots.

Therefore, a fundamental objective in creating new urban structures and in renovating and improving old ones is to combine an evolution of traditional elements with radically new architectural models. This objective is easily understood but difficult to bring about, and nowadays the theory and practice of the most demanding kind of urban development revolves around this difficulty.

The fact that within the last decade the city of Barcelona has broken the inertia with many examples of urban design, from pocket parks to renovated but integrated mixed-use districts like the Olympic Village, and greened traffic links that have made the metropolitan city understandable, stands as an example of this new approach to urban design, an understanding of the city which has an eminent capacity to be translated to other corners of European culture.

If we take a closer look at what is taking place in Temple Bar, we will discover that the functional city is a virtual vision far from the reality of casual encounters of the accidental process of continual renovation. The real function of the city depends on its diversity of people, ideas and aspirations, for which its urban design must allow. Diversity began with Group 91, a get-together of eight young architectural practices who won the urban design competition back in 1991. The group character of this combined practice implied a discussion of ideas and conflicting solutions which gave life to the project, just like the city itself.

The immediate construction of some of the buildings and public spaces allowed Dubliners to participate and criticise, remembering that one is only critical of something if one is interested – sometimes passionately – in something cherished. A balance between leisure pursuits of bars and restaurants and new small-scale accommodation for housing and offices is holding the stage for casual encounters together. The same must be hoped for cars and people: neither should be excluded.

But the Liffey should not be a barrier and the Ha'penny Bridge needs the partner that was proposed by the 91 team to link with Ormond Quay so that some of the enthusiasm of Temple Bar could spill over to the other side. The renewal of Temple Bar must not contain itself with hard edges converting it into a cultural ghetto. Therefore its vital energy and qualities of urban design must be allowed to cross the road and river and sow the seed of the young and happily conflictive quarter elsewhere.

I believe that we can stroll over the Liffey and wander through the lanes of Temple Bar and find, with Seamus Heaney, a future affirming itself under our feet.

DAVID MACKAY is a writer and lecturer on architectural and urban subjects. He has been practicing architecture for nearly 40 years in Barcelona with his partners Josep Martorell and Oriol Bohigas. The team is probably best-known for the urban design of the Olympic Village and Port in 1992.

Living Over The Shop

FRANK McDONALD

THERE'S NOTHING VERY NOVEL ABOUT THE IDEA OF LIVING OVER THE SHOP. IT USED TO be the norm in cities and towns all over Ireland, as elsewhere in Europe, when the proverbial butchers, bakers and candlestick-makers all lived above their own business premises in the main trading streets. But that was before railways, tram lines and, ultimately, cars encouraged a mass migration from the city to the suburbs. Lock-up shops became the new standard, more often than not secured by alarms and aluminium shutters, and the upper floor space degenerated into storage use – if, indeed, it was used at all.

It took a long time, and a virtual sea-change in public policy, before there was any recognition that this wasted space represented a major potential asset, particularly for reversion to residential use. Because not only would this help bring life back to town centres, it would also arrest the decay of historic buildings.

On the Continent, it is still commonplace to find numerous apartments above shops, even in the main streets of cities and towns. In Paris, the quintessential European city, there is a symbiotic relationship between the survival of the boulangeries, charcuteries and patisseries and the continued existence of a residential population in the city centre. Street after street, the upper floors of most Parisian shop buildings are occupied by a healthy mix of architects' offices, doctors' surgeries and miscellaneous other uses, including apartments large and small. As a result, the street never dies; there are always enough people around, even after dark, to sustain the corner grocery and *bar tabac*. As Jonathan Glancey noted in the *Independent on*

Padania, a new Italian delicatessen in Spranger's Yard (Burke Kennedy Doyle Architects)

opposite
The Cobbles, East Essex Street (Douglas Wallace Opperman Architects)

Sunday in 1991, 'They survive not just because they are wanted, but because most are small, family businesses and, in Paris, a small family business pays very little in the way of local rates and taxes ... The shops are handed down through families and so maintain their independent existence.' What's more, there is a real determination to ensure that they survive. Under municipal law, which some might think draconian, a butcher who decides to sell his business can only sell it to another butcher; the same rule would apply to a hairdresser, a café owner, a *pattisier* or any other trade or service deemed vital to the life of a neighbourhood.

Such interference with the market would be unimaginable in Ireland. Yet along with the survival of a residential community, it helps to explain why the market streets of Paris still prosper, while London's have been 'consigned to the history books or else pickled in theme-park aspic, as, for example, in Covent Garden', as Glancey wrote. 'Where Londoners are faced with high streets lined with banks, building societies, estate agents and video shops, are bullied by massive American-style shopping malls and virtually forced into supermarkets (excellent though they may be), Parisians can buy a bag of nails or 100 grammes of *marrons glacées* from a shop around the corner.'

The proliferation of supermarkets and purpose-built shopping centres, in Dublin as well as London, has killed the corner shop. Small, family-run businesses cannot compete, or survive, in a retail culture dominated by bulk-buying high street multiples and the car-borne customers they are geared to serve. And this results in the death of the street.

It is the inevitable consequence of suburbanisation and the adoption of suburban 'values'. Add to this the horror with which pension funds, insurance companies and other property investors view the very idea of mixed-use buildings and it becomes easy to explain why there is almost nobody living in Grafton Street or Henry Street, for example. The financial institutions, who now have a virtual stranglehold on the ownership of property in Dublin's premier retail streets, would much prefer the upper floors to remain empty than be converted to residential use. As one of their investment managers once said, 'There's no guarantee that one of the flats wouldn't be turned into a brothel.'

In the secondary shopping streets, which are of little interest to the institutions, there is more hope of a residential revival. But it is only since 1989, when York-based Ann Petherick launched her Living Over The Shop (LOTS) campaign, that the authorities in Britain, and later Ireland, began to see that this notion might have some potential.

Petherick's initiative snowballed. From 1990, when the British Government's Housing Corporation provided £300,000 to fund three pilot projects, the finance available grew to £12 million in 1993 and she was working with no less than 300 local authorities – clearly indicating that Living Over The Shop was an idea whose time had come.

Though initially sceptical when it was first suggested here, senior officials of the Department of the Environment began to sit up and take notice. Finally, in the 1994 Budget, a special scheme of incentives was announced to encourage residential conversions of the upper floors of shop buildings in 'designated streets', such as Capel Street.

The scheme has not been a success. For a start, it was based on a belief that ordinary shopkeepers would be immediately tempted to become property developers, merely to avail of the tax incentives on offer. This proved to be mistaken, as the very disappointing level of take-up in the designated streets clearly demonstrates. Secondly, the Government's involvement was limited to tax incentives; unlike Britain, no grants were made available. Thirdly, the scheme is not attractive to end-users because it is limited to refurbished buildings, which means that first-time purchasers not only lose a £3,000 grant, but also have to pay the severe penalty of stamp duty. Fourthly, the scheme was bedevilled by unresolved problems relating to fire safety and the onerous need to comply with Building Regulations which impose late-20th-century standards on pre-existing buildings. And finally, the relatively undeveloped voluntary housing sector showed little inclination to intervene in this area.

The latter is an important consideration. Because if the LOTS scheme was tailored to suit rented accommodation rather than owners or investors, the voluntary housing associations, such as Focus Point, might be able to use the grant-aid which it receives to convert vacant floor space to residential use, instead of leaving it to the shopkeeper.

One of the main reasons why LOTS has worked in Temple Bar is that the development of the area is overseen by a single-purpose agency. Temple Bar Properties was able to purchase the entire CIÉ property portfolio, and made a number of other acquisitions, enabling it to develop new mixed-use buildings or refurbish existing buildings for LOTS schemes. In some of these cases, the buildings were admittedly gutted and their interiors rebuilt, including the provision of fire-proof concrete floor slabs to separate a shop or restaurant at street level from apartments overhead. This is not analogous to shopkeepers in, say, Capel Street who might wish to provide flats on the upper floors while they continued trading.

The first LOTS scheme in Temple Bar – indeed, in the centre of Dublin – was pioneered by Bríd and Gerry Dukes, at the corner of Dame Street and Parliament Street, in 1989. Without the benefit of tax incentives, they created the Riverrun Gallery at street level, a restaurant upstairs and a duplex apartment overhead to live in with their family. Their example was followed in 1991 by Colman Ó Siochrú, a young Dublin architect. With financial support from his uncle, he bought No.35 Parliament Street and converted the upper floors into four apartments, including one for himself. Not long afterwards, in a joint venture with Temple Bar Properties, his elder sister, Emer Ó Siochrú, did the same with the former Royal Exchange Hotel across the street. By then, of course, there were generous tax incentives available and Temple Bar was beginning to take off. Parliament Street had been brought back from the dead.

None of this would have happened if CIÉ had not behaved so responsibly when it was acquiring the core of the area for its transportation centre. By letting its buildings rather than blocking them up, it unwittingly facilitated the emergence of Temple Bar as Dublin's 'left bank' with art galleries, funky clothes shops and rock band rehearsal studios.

Many of the new retail units in Temple Bar are restaurants or pubs, rather than shops as such. Indeed, part of what makes the area so attractive to visitors is the almost unlimited variety of its restaurants, pubs and nightclubs which suggest that it is fast replacing such old haunts as Leeson Street as Dublin's 'Night-town'. Living over the shop is one thing; living over a noisy pub is quite another. In 1995, after the Temple Bar Residents Association expressed its fear that the area was in danger of being turned into a 'drinking mall', agreement was reached with certain publicans to restrict the phenomenon of on-street drinking, in everyone else's interest.

Temple Bar has deservedly won awards for the quality of so many of its LOTS schemes – notably the Printworks (by Derek Tynan Architects) which won the Architectural Association of Ireland's Downes Medal in 1995, not least because it offered a new model for city-centre living, with apartments arranged around a courtyard at first-floor level.

Another Temple Bar Properties development, the Granary, in which I am privileged to live, won an RIAI Regional Award for Peter Twamley for the quality of its refurbishment, which created five generously-sized, loft-style apartments and a large communal roof terrace over three shop units at street level. For me, it is the epitome of city-centre living, the realisation of a dream. The real luxury of living in Temple Bar means a

four-minute walk to work – or two minutes by bicycle, if I'm in a rush – or being able to nip out at any time of the day or night to get a pint of milk or anything else we might require. And if the fridge is empty, all we need to do is walk out onto the street and drop into any one of the numerous restaurants. But there is one, perhaps unforeseen, consequence of living in the city centre – one's whole world seems to contract. Because everything is available, from the proverbial needle-to-anchor, one tends to stay well inside the canal ring. Even going out to Ranelagh for dinner becomes something of an adventure, while Killiney seems to be on another planet.

In *The Destruction of Dublin*, I wrote about the 'potentially delightful area under the menacing shadow of the Central Bank', and suggested that it could be 'Dublin's answer to Greenwich Village in New York or the Marais quarter of Paris', with people living in refurbished buildings tucked away in its network of narrow streets. Now I'm right in the middle of it all.

However, the jury is still out on whether Temple Bar can retain the 'alternative' character which saved it from demolition for CIÉ's transportation centre. The policy of selling off shop/restaurant units to private investors, rather than retaining effective State control into the future, could ultimately lead to its absorption into the high-street retail zone. And that would be a pity.

PS – I never thought I would end up living above a gentleman's cosmetic shop!

FRANK McDONALD is Environment Correspondent of *The Irish Times*, and has written extensively about Temple Bar since 1982. He is also the author of *The Destruction of Dublin* (Gill & Macmillan, Dublin, 1985) and *Saving the City* (Tomar, Dublin, 1989).

An apartment in the refurbished Granary building, Temple Lane (Peter Twamley Architect)

Dublin Masque

SIMON WALKER

THE TEMPLE BAR PROJECT RAISES AS MANY QUESTIONS AS IT answers, about the meaning of urban renewal, the approach to renovating the city, the new architecture, how the future of Dublin is taking shape, what it will contain. But to define one's own position in relation to the politics of urban renewal, or to arrive at a critical evaluation of the architecture, it is necessary to consider the truth of the urban story, to separate myth from reality, to understand the context in which this new architecture has come about. How does the expression of the new architecture represent renewal? How does it succeed in repossessing the public space?

VERNACULAR AND MASQUE

A pattern had been established since the early Middle Ages in Dublin, linking the *frons scenae* of important buildings with 'vernacular' infill. When, in the seventeenth century, James Butler, Duke of Ormonde, laid out the first quay, Ormonde Quay, this was the point at which Dublin really began to develop the notion of the public face of the city. The political imperative behind the making of this public architecture, in particular the quay-front, was the creation of a public space which would represent both government and private citizen. For the next 150 years, public and private building tended to project this demonstrative element, this public face, a wrap-around façade to the public space of the city. While the architectural language, or style, of this façade became High Classicism in the eighteenth century, the essential component of the public buildings was not a classical concern with structure or engineering, but a more staged, Baroque sense of theatricality. Each public façade had an internal symmetry and a preconceived relationship to a streetscape or urban vista, each building played a role in a kind of urban theatre. I like to refer to this notion of the city as an architectural 'masque', a word meaning the kind of courtly spectacle or drama in vogue at the time, but coming from the masks worn by the actors, or 'company of maskers'. In the same way, the buildings adopted a public, decorative mask which effectively disguised their true structural nature.

Temple Bar Square (Group 91 / Grafton Architects)

TRUTH AND PRETENCE

In the layout and expression of this modern city there remained, however, a similar proportional relationship to a simple and unpretentious vernacular fabric which had existed in the old city. A constant tension, or balance, existed between the 'pretence' of the masque and the 'truth' of the vernacular, between the carved stone temple-front and the terraced house. Certainly, 'truth' in building stimulates architectural development; by searching to remain true to the science of construction, architecture bestows a legacy of lasting quality, and may succeed in expanding the possibilities of form. But the masque represents the political act of building, and therefore mediates the understanding by the public of the urban context.

In recent decades, the relationship between masque and vernacular has become completely reversed. Public buildings, or institutional buildings which should have been public, lost their ability to perform or mediate in public, while the characteristic appearance of eighteenth-century vernacular has been abducted into a grotesque mask in order to conceal modern truths of construction. To this day, there is precious little consensus on the political act of building – the bourgeoisie, if such a term can still be applied, is divided and confused; the rest of society is mostly unrepresented. How can we make a critical evaluation of Dublin's new architecture in the absence of such a consensus?

GROUND AND FACE

Two areas of analysis inform us of the public's relation to architecture: common ground and public face. By 'ground', I do not just mean site; I mean the social and cultural background from whence the architecture of our buildings evolved. The ground of architecture is the perceived shared basis on which we form our response to architecture, and it includes collective memory and mythology. Dublin is unusual because it is the seat of power of the nation, yet its public squares, streets and houses are the built legacy of the colonial power that not so long ago denied that very nation's existence. The absence of an appropriate symbolic place or assimilation for Dublin into the culture makes the ground for the repossession of public space very uneasy and shifting. There is, at best, ambivalence, at worst, deep mistrust, about the notion of owning the city of tall houses and public buildings. Even O'Connell Street, a possible focus for civic pride, feels instead like one of the ravaged arteries of Belgrade or Bucharest. Not publicly ostentatious, the people of Dublin are renowned for their backroom humour, their subversion, their disappearing acts. The real expression of the city's culture is to be found in these private spaces.

But in the 1990s, an emerging Euro-consciousness has become evident, a will to make something of the urban centre. American-style suburbia may still be the ideal for many, but there is a definite shift in investment into the city centre, although, as yet, the infrastructure, commerce and planning of this developmental trend is largely chaotic. At the end of a century which has known traumatic changes for Dublin and the island as a whole, we have finally come to face realistically the question of our relationship to the city. Now we have an opportunity to stabilise the future of the city. Instead of herd-like behaviour dictated by seemingly arbitrary planning or over-simplistic market analysis, rather than jumping from one mass demographic upheaval of biblical proportions to another, we should by now be able to hold our ground and let services and businesses adapt themselves to work around us.

The environment is now perhaps the single most important factor guiding local authority planning decisions. However the concept of 'environment' is not often that of a new and vibrant urbane culture as artists and architects would have wished, but instead it is a world of heavily controlled fakery and pastiche. There is little evidence of a new language, of modern 'truths' of building, of an attempt to reveal or indeed 'interpret' what is contained in the context, merely a general-adherence to an arbitrary and debased language of reproduction.

The reasons for this apparent failure are various, but paramount among them is the relationship between architects and the building industry. In Ireland, the use of professional architects on construction projects is not a mandatory requirement, with the result that, until a recent perceptible shift, architects were peripheral to the industry – an 'extra'. This is borne out by the Department of the Environment figures for the percentage of private estate housing involving architects: ten years ago it was 4%, lately it has climbed to 17%. So, in effect, the planners' main work has been to provide a guidance service to engineers and builders for the most part. In the absence of any 'architectural' attitude or training, their retreat into the familiarity of an imagined past reflects the innate conservatism of the builders. At the end of this unfortunate process, the end-users are those who are least well served, who have the least imaginative range of options. But if we are to improve on this situation, the solution will not come from architects alone; obviously, it must involve developers also.

This is the 'ground' on which the present wave of new architecture has come ashore. Perhaps part of the rationale behind the development of a 'cultural quarter', behind so-called urban renewal, is the same as that behind the development of visitor/interpretative centres, rural job-creation programmes, even some inner-city job-creation programmes: tourism. Unless we are to give our country over to tourist kitsch, obviously development cannot be simply physical, it must also be cultural and intellectual, it must involve both architecture and building. And it is possible to infer that it was this reason, which may be called the 'cultural imperative', which necessitated direct government intervention in the case of Temple Bar, in order to break the deadening cycle of the planning/development process.

The retained façade of Designyard

The Development Programme for Temple Bar, initiated by Temple Bar Properties Ltd, a government-owned company, has, from the beginning, encountered widespread mistrust, and equally widespread enthusiasm. Both have been heightened by the fact that the first phase of the development has not been finished until now. As we have seen, there are psychological reasons for this mistrust, and so we have to address the problem of the city's past, the ground, but also the face: how do we relate to the public face that is in the city's architecture? Duality has always been a feature of Dublin; some would even call it duplicity. There is a face and an obverse, which can neither be separated nor can they look at each other. The face is a continuous lacework of brick and stone, archways, string-courses and cornices; the obverse is the story of the overcrowding, neglect and eventual abandonment. But while the historical face is grudgingly appreciated, even loved, the notion of creating a new contemporary face is shied away from. Yet creating one's own architectural 'face' is the only way to confirm our cultural identity and assert ownership of the public realm. Redefining the urban involves not just the architecture itself, but includes the relationship, the 'interface'; between architecture and user. Only when we get past nostalgia and sentimentality will we be able to create an architecture that is of our own time, that represents and does not betray.

FAÇADE

If we look at a cross-section of the public street, the psychological and physical problem of repossession is reduced to one critical band-width: the façade. In the aftermath of such a crisis of identity as Dublin has suffered, it is the façade which exercises both the Corporation and the public minds; this is what I call 'the problem of skin'. The new buildings on Temple Bar Square by Grafton Architects, and McCullough Mulvin's Temple Bar Gallery and Studios and Black Church Print Studio, make no apologies for their obvious enjoyment of the exploitation of skin. Skin becomes 'masque', in the theatrical sense, not in a craven, false attempt to hide structure, which is the case with the ubiquitous new concrete-frame office and apartment buildings clad in a single thickness of stretcher-bonded brick. The new Temple Bar buildings listed above are instead a deliberate composition closer to the manipulative nature of the Baroque, a playful kind of expression, informed by the 1920s and 1930s Bauhaus designs. Taking advantage of the possibilities of modern construction, these buildings make clear the separation of skin and structure, and brick veneer is contained in steel-framed panels. Glazing has a horizontal emphasis, as befits concrete-frame buildings, and there is an obvious delight in the treatment of the window units and wall surfaces. So although the façades of these buildings are exhibitionist, or playful, they do not attempt to hide their structural nature.

The surprise of seeing a contemporary building without any of the usual kitsch touches – such as little painted balconies, 20mm granite facing on the ground floor, brick pediments and brass gimmickry – is a pleasure not just for people in the area, but for the city in general. Temple Bar Gallery and Studios engages the reinforced concrete frame of an existing early twentieth-century industrial building on the site – these buildings survive throughout the area – providing a bold, striking corner to Temple Bar Square, and, perhaps more importantly, is the best piece of new infill yet on the quays behind. Inside, there is a stripped-down aesthetic – exposed electrics, concrete floors – which is appropriate to its post-industrial use. The building does just what one would expect of a modern building: it provides strong floors, large expanses of glass, easy access and a varied and useful roof deck. It, and other new buildings in the area, also operate on the level of sheer enjoyment of modern, mostly inexpensive, materials such as profiled metal sheeting, steel doors, etched glass and drywall interiors.

OLD AND NEW

A building has no inherent worth or beauty unless it represents the best efforts of people, technology, and indigenous culture at any given time. Buildings, like all art, are a contemporaneous record of a civilisation. We have permitted a phoney image of Dublin to come about and have ignored the potential of what it actually contains. But clichés such as the nostalgic interiors of 'Timber Tinseltown' public houses, most of which are reconstructions, have little to do with contemporary culture. Local authorities everywhere may realise that their areas are better served by the informed use of architecture rather than wasting resources in a prolonged battle over architectural language and favouring formula-based development corporations who do not use architects.

Two lessons to be learned from the emerging architecture of Temple Bar are, firstly, that people are best served in 1996 as they were in 1796 – by an architecture that is the best, most innovative, most honest, most forward-looking, most sensitive and most technically proficient of its time. Secondly, the completed buildings prove that modern architectural language can exist in a happy and vibrant symbiosis with that of two centuries earlier. In other words, respect for context means respect for scale, use, street layout and the social contract a building must have with its immediate area, as distinct from the imposition of a shallow and nasty pastiche which leaves the city a cultural backwater.

Of course, planning policy must take the utmost care to preserve the (genuine) ancient fabric, yet allow the ancient to co-exist with the best of modern architecture. The effect is to enhance both, and to predicate a consistently varied and evolving urban pattern. Other key elements contribute to the survival and growth of the city centre: widespread residential use, a riverscape and quayside which become an integral precinct for pedestrian use (any meaningful circuit taking in the northside needs another pedestrian bridge) and efficient and unobtrusive public transport.

Hegel asked, 'Is architecture everything that is not building?', referring to an architectural 'supplement' which applies to the base material – its vernacular. If the vernacular is the 'text' of building, then the masque, the public architecture, is its literature, its grand fiction. The play between masque and vernacular is enriched by proposing new language, new iconographies and new physical configurations as continuations of the urban theatre, or as instruments of communicating a sense of place. When people refer to 'visionary architecture' they may well be talking about the 18th century, a time when the spirit of building in Dublin epitomised 'a simple and pure love for an unknown future'. It must do so again.

REVOLUTION AND IDENTITY

Where do the new buildings of Temple Bar stand in relation to this need for a liberation of spirit; how do they fulfil their 'cultural' brief? To what extent is what Marcuse calls the 'sensuous substance of the Beautiful' preserved in the public works which are overtly designed to produce such reactions as admiration, to appear impressive, beautiful? Where does the concept of 'beautiful' stand in relation to the opposition of pretence to truth? The twentieth-century experience of art as it moved beyond the picture frame, from representational to non-objective art and an engagement with the gallery space and eventually with the viewer directly, has provided the example for modernism in architecture. The tools – signs, representations – with which the artist/architect mediates reality have been given a new territory: the blank white page, the white cube, the neutral space. This space demands to be

colonised by a new visual language (or languages), in turn demanded by new mental landscapes. This new colony permits, even requires, the liberalisation of all former constraints. This liberalising process is achieved by the artist through all the media of art, including building.

But if building is a political act, then the modern architect is involved in the politics of revolution. The revolution affords the mental and political space for the establishment of new identities, the search for which was the underlying cause of revolution, and is at the core of all art. But how does the architect avoid the predictable ideological compromises of building, of association with money and power? If architecture becomes merely a service industry for the wealthy, then pretence may take over completely from truth, and the artistic tension necessary for the beautiful to exist will be gone. Architects must remain true to their own work, dealing foremost with the communication of design concepts, which are the production of the mind.

If revolution means the search for identity, is it valid to try to claim or establish a 'national' architectural identity? If we look at the work of James Joyce, we can see that certain mental processes, evolved from specific conditions of place, can inform the artistic impetus to create work which is universal, which reaches beyond the confines of that place, and which reciprocates by revolutionising that place. Joyce has introduced the Irish people to the genius of comedy arising from within their own culture. This he has done by exploding artistic conventions and creating authentic art. Moreover, in *Ulysses* he imagines a revolutionary, modern Dublin, fragmented, self-aware, and lampoons the Gaelic Revival attempts at retrogression. Ed Jones asks, 'Is eclecticism the natural inheritor of the Irish tradition?' But mere eclecticism does not revolutionise; it retreats. Joyce's work goes beyond the ethnic or place-specific classification contained in eclecticism; it deconstructs; it is autonomous form; it is 'art for art's sake'. The Dublin that Joyce dreamed of has not yet assumed possession of the space of public appearance, but the Temple Bar work of O'Donnell and Tuomey, the arch of the Photography Archive, the composition of the IFC, McCullough Mulvin's planning of the Black Church Print Studio, Grafton Architect's dissociation of the Temple Bar Square façade, and Shay Cleary's Curved Street tend towards subversion, self-reference, and autonomy of form.

THE PLEASURE PRINCIPLE

Current research in architectural drawing into mapping, fragmentation, overlay, and the dissolution of formal style, have offered architects encouragement for experimentation. The critic Manfredo Tafuri, claims that 'turning architecture upside-down renders legitimate the sinking into the bottomless well of the autonomy of form', and that 'the pleasure of subtle mental games that subjugate the absoluteness of forms' has no social value. I disagree. The combined pressure of questioning, experimental, critical work does produce major sea-changes in architecture – work, including the unbuilt work of Group 91 such as *Making a Modern Street*,[1] which, all taken together, has shown the way forward from the doldrums of the late seventies and early eighties. Joyce's autonomy of form had a positive, creative agenda. He was not limited within the structures of language itself, nor attempting to subvert a syntactical code from within; he was drawing on a local/colloquial source, spoken words and sounds, collective memory. His invention was to facilitate a *remenagement* of all sensory experience. As in Joyce, the new architecture uses deconstruction to reconstruct.

Do we have to transgress the limits of convention in Dublin's architecture – as Joyce did in literature – in order to find its ultimate pleasure? Bernard Tschumi's defence of the 'pleasure' rationale allows a redefinition of masque. He acknowledges that the sensual experience of a building, or an architectural space, is a concrete, subjective, human activity. But only by simultaneously being aware of the architectural 'rule', or logic, is the subject able to lose the gap between sensory pleasure and reason, to reach the depth of sensuality. 'Architecture needs both system and excess,' says Tschumi. Likewise the urban fabric. He quotes Roland Barthes: 'In the text of pleasure, the opposing forces are no longer repressed but in a state of becoming.' It reads like the perfect equation for the urban renewal of Dublin.

OBJECT AND SUBJECT

The subjective 'perception' of physical space is coloured by a number of factors – memory, context, interpretation – which are therefore outside the logic of architectural form-making, but inescapably part of the individual user's reaction/participation, no less so than the individual architect's creative process. Therefore, in order to maintain the balance between subject and object, between vernacular and masque, between the ostentatious and the mundane, the architectural conception underlying the framework plan for the area had to demonstrate a sensitivity and an understanding of the human response. Alongside the revolutionary freedom and the pleasure espoused in the re-invention of the public masque, there must exist a level of architectural detail which is the key to the sustainability of the area.

A review of the competition entries for the framework plan in 1991 shows the Group 91 scheme as the most 'devolved' in this respect, eschewing as it does the 'master-plan' method, no doubt because of the architects' familiarity with the thinking behind 'human-scale development'. Many of them studied at the RCA, London, in the 1970s under Leon Krier, at a time when notions such as 'living over the shop' and the reintegration of the urban centre with its mediaeval past were fundamental positions of post-Modernist thinking. Derek Tynan studied at Cornell University with Colin Rowe, proposer of the 'scaffold-and-exhibit' vision of urban planning which described a happy and invigorating relationship between old and new. This teaching found a sympathetic audience in Dublin, among many other non-Group 91 architects of that generation as well, some of whom have produced work in Temple Bar. An exhibition of Irish architecture, mostly 'paper projects', entitled *Traditions and Directions*, shown at the ICA, London, in 1980, further propagated an alternative, contextualist approach to new architecture and urban planning. Since those often bitter times of recession and heated polemic, Group 91's work generally has become fresher and more liberated, but it is this background nevertheless, and their ability to articulate an underlying philosophy of contextual sensitivity, that appears to have coincided exactly with what the Government wanted to achieve in Temple Bar.

The Temple Bar project has allowed the release of cultural expression in the conception of appropriately scaled public buildings and spaces, but also has set sustainable and informed precedents for the re-inhabitation of the city centre. Contained in the development are relatively mundane, but often ingenious, elements of architecture that act as prototypes, as we can see in the example of Tynan's Printworks apartment building. The moves that must be clearly present in a coherent urban plan are generative moves, infrastructural moves, that come directly from a late twentieth-century understanding of the needs of a modern city: the development of courtyard spaces, the balance of a critical level of density with a wide range of living spaces – duplex and triplex apartments, loft spaces, open-air terraces – the maintenance of a minimum number of storeys, the development of basement spaces, the integration of residential and commercial uses, with service access for commercial units and off-street parking for residences, as well as the technical expertise required to provide successful soundproofing and protected and well-lit access to apartments within buildings, stairways and lifts.

It is clear that we are no longer constrained to enter musty debates about what is or what is not Irish culture, what is art and what is not, nor even what are the criteria for a 'native' architecture. These are all didactic impulses which try to prescribe 'legitimate' fields of cultural activity. Irish people have found their voice – literature and music are not the only arts – and now there is a widespread redefinition of subject/object in all the arts. The presence of multi-media centres is telling in itself, and indeed, *The Power of an Idea* exhibition tried to dissolve the rigidity of pre-existing architectural presentation formats in order to better reveal process and motive. A sign of growing maturity is that people have trust in our artists, and, perhaps belatedly, our architects, believing that what they create does represent the 'truths' of modern society.

[1] Group 91, *Making a Modern Street* (Gandon Editions, 1991)

SIMON WALKER is an architect and critic. He teaches at UCD School of Architecture and also works in private practice. He was the curator of *The Power of an Idea*, an architectural exhibition held in Temple Bar in July 1996 to celebrate the completion of Phase 1 of the development project.

On reading
Temple Bar

DECLAN McGONAGLE

TO ADDRESS THE TEMPLE BAR PROJECT AS A WHOLE AND NOT to simply review its individual elements is analogous to addressing Ireland and its position within our own minds and the imagination of others at the end of the 20th century. For it is only in this, the last decade of the century, that those emancipating forces which were seeded in the 1960s in Ireland have crystallised and are now visible in a variety of contexts and processes in Irish society, of which Temple Bar is one of the primary examples.

There are, of course, several strands of activity in Temple Bar whose conception and realisation deserve their own documentation, analysis and evaluation, but Temple Bar is not just innovative urbanism or property development, economic regeneration or a series of cultural initiatives. It is both a reflection of and a contribution to contemporary Irish society, and ultimately has to be tested as such.

Its reading, therefore, cannot be limited to the limitations of any single strand of its programme. It is not a question of good or bad buildings or spaces, or of specific projects recognisable as art, but of a holistic enterprise whose composite totality is more than the sum of its parts.

While Temple Bar is not the first nor the biggest culture-led urban renewal project in the Euro-American environment, it is the first model in Ireland which has a conscious attitude to the nature and meaning of living within a city and its values, without denial of what was in place before.

It is related to but quite unlike the other moment in real time in the 1960s when forces of material regeneration were also consciously unlocked in Ireland. The difference is that the idea of change then was localised in manifestations of modernism projected as *replacements* of what had gone before. Temple Bar represents coexistence and a composite reality which is capable of expressing new states of mind being formulated in Ireland in the nineties. Where the sixties was probably the last moment in this century, in Ireland and else-

Arthouse, the multi-media centre for the arts
on Curved Street
(Group 91 / Shay Cleary Architects)

where, where a belief in linear progress was tenable – in effect religious belief disguised as secular thought – Temple Bar represents the idea that it is possible (and I would argue necessary) to occupy and act in several fields simultaneously. However, we should be as careful of the label of post-Modernism as of Modernism, for one is the product of the other, and neither will serve. It may be convenient shorthand to utilise such thinking and naming, but the composite rather than the singular reality being articulated and acknowledged in our wider society actually predates the Modernism of the 19th and 20th centuries. This was driven by the particular forces of industrial capitalism with which this country has had a peripheral relationship, which marginalised the Irish economy, and valued ancient rather than contemporary visual culture.

It is also no coincidence that the mid-1960s saw attempts at industrialisation, disastrous urban development (not unique to Ireland), the fiftieth commemoration of the Rising, and an attempt by Seán Lemass to renegotiate the relationship between north and south. But the force that was defined as desirable, underpinning all of this modernisation, amounted to a tardy, gestural mimicry of Modernism, which was a mere patina, like perspex shopfronts, on Irish society, politics and culture, as if it were possible to modernise (even accepting that it was beneficial) a country/society simply by changing how it looked rather than how it thought.

Despite initiatives by individuals or groups, the whole society had not gone through a process of renegotiation with itself, and was locked in denial of the complexities of its composite identity. Deep-seated foundation myths have only recently been reconsidered as a direct result of the uncomfortable questions raised by The Troubles in the North and the re-reading of ourselves as European, with the latter having a direct bearing on material support essential to projects like Temple Bar. In the context of urban/cultural space, what was previously true of planning, true of architecture and true of art is not true of Temple Bar and the urban/cultural space it created and now occupies. There are real dangers if other similarly scaled developments are not also driven by an integrated, holistic approach.

We know that a process of denial is common to all colonised and post-colonial situations, where certain processes are almost automatically rejected from the social/political body and others adopted. In the Irish process, denial led to headline urban development, albeit on a relatively small scale, at the cost of previous histories, previous architecture, and to the emergence of the scabs of Modernism aligned with corporate projection known as public sculpture.

If Temple Bar's public art projects have seemed incidental so far, that is because its essential dynamic does not lie in discrete art projects. The 'art' in Temple Bar lies in the relationships between individual buildings, the total environment, social space and the attendant public transactions within the city. Since these have to do with the reintegration of culture with social interaction, they cannot be judged in aesthetic terms alone.

It has been well argued elsewhere that Temple Bar includes all the elements of urban regeneration, cultural initiatives and public art, but it is the combination of these elements and Temple Bar's composite nature, originating in the instinctive and unsentimental economic action of artists, which amounts to a summary of the issues – dangers as well as opportunities – which face Ireland at the end of the 20th century.

It has become possible in this decade to consider other readings and to acknowledge that Ireland is a composite, that layers of meaning do exist in this environment, and, crucially, to act politically, socially and culturally upon that understanding. To read Temple Bar, therefore, is to read Ireland, with Cromwell's warts, carbuncles and all.

DECLAN McGONAGLE was appointed the first director of the Irish Museum of Modern Art, which was established by the Irish government in 1990 and opened in 1991. He was formerly Director of the Orchard Gallery in Derry and Director of Exhibitions at the Institute of Contemporary Arts in London. In 1987 he was nominated for the Turner Prize for making the Orchard Gallery an international centre for the artist. He has served on various public bodies and juries, and lectures regularly on contemporary visual art issues.

opposite

top – The Artifact database on Irish artists

bottom left – The Artifact Kiosk at Arthouse

bottom right – Cyberia, the Internet café in Arthouse

Jim Buckley

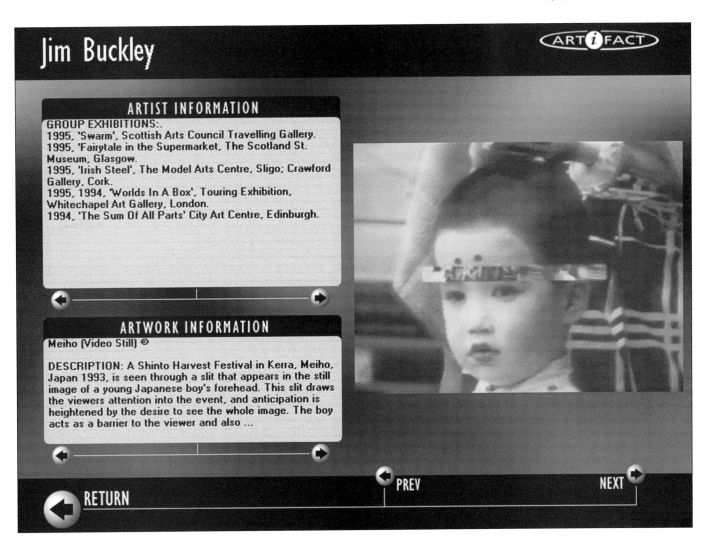

ARTIST INFORMATION

GROUP EXHIBITIONS:.
1995, 'Swarm', Scottish Arts Council Travelling Gallery.
1995, 'Fairytale in the Supermarket, The Scotland St. Museum, Glasgow.
1995, 'Irish Steel', The Model Arts Centre, Sligo; Crawford Gallery, Cork.
1995, 1994, 'Worlds In A Box', Touring Exhibition, Whitechapel Art Gallery, London.
1994, 'The Sum Of All Parts' City Art Centre, Edinburgh.

ARTWORK INFORMATION

Meiho (Video Still) ⊚

DESCRIPTION: A Shinto Harvest Festival in Kerra, Meiho, Japan 1993, is seen through a slit that appears in the still image of a young Japanese boy's forehead. This slit draws the viewers attention into the event, and anticipation is heightened by the desire to see the whole image. The boy acts as a barrier to the viewer and also ...

PREV   NEXT

RETURN

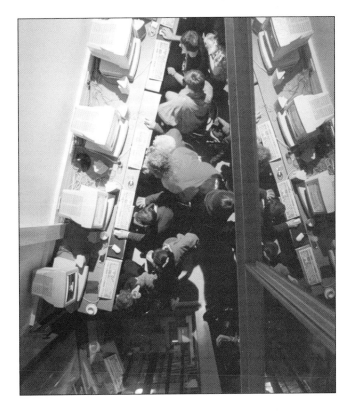

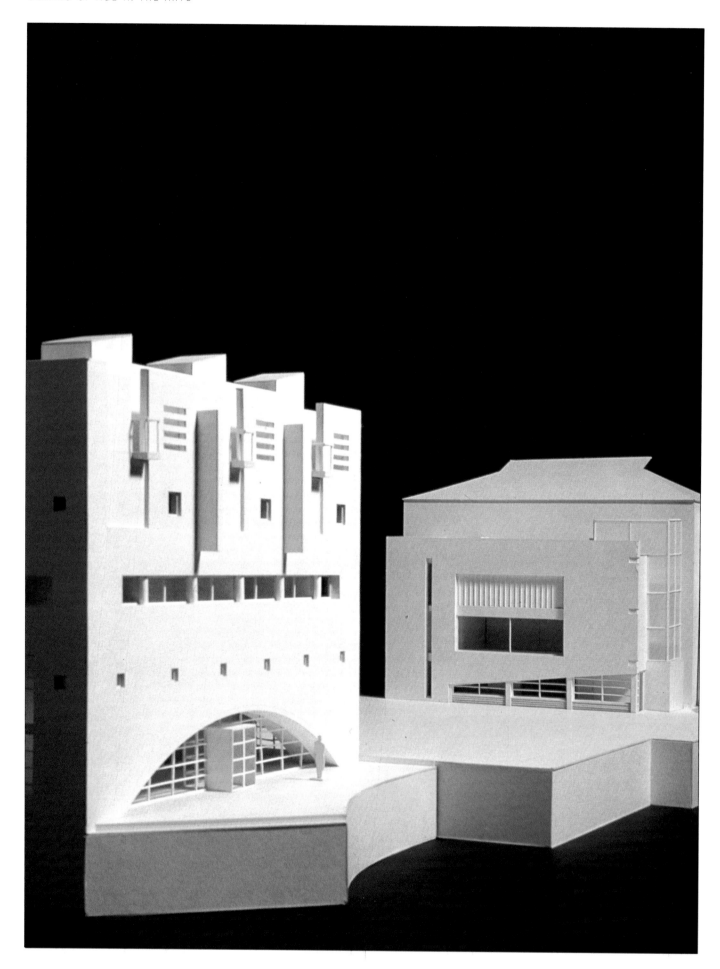

Coming of Age in the Arts

THE CHALLENGES IMPOSED BY TEMPLE BAR'S
CULTURAL PROGRAMME

COLM Ó BRIAIN in conversation with Helen Meany

*Helen Meany – What is your evaluation of the cultural programme of Temple Bar
Properties so far?*

COLM Ó BRIAIN – THE CULTURAL DIMENSION OF THE TEMPLE BAR PROJECT REPRE-
sents a quantum leap from what preceded it. It has provided a new infrastructure for the city and a level of facilities with which many contemporary arts practitioners and managers have not been familiar. Previously,
the norm would have been a small arts organisation working on a limited revenue
budget in an inadequate building. In Temple Bar, ad hoc organisations had slipped
into the area under the CIÉ remit, found an empty building, adapted it to their purpose and lobbied for short-term funding. The idea of developing a cultural infrastructure, of providing buildings that catered for the needs of organisations, was in
some ways an uncomfortable development for arts administrators, artists and the
voluntary committees representing artists. It required a sea-change in people's
thinking, a new comprehension of the changed context in which they were going to
do their work in future. It also meant growing up. Under the 'leaking building' ordi-
nance, there had been lots of goodwill towards artists and a sense of surviving in
adversity. Audiences made allowances; art was being made *despite* the buildings
in which the work was housed. But where the infrastructure is in place, one expects
better delivery of the finished artistic project. Therefore, one doesn't make compen-
sations when coming to a judgement.

This is the essence of the change for all of the cultural organisations working in the
Temple Bar area. They are graduating into a new context, which will pose quite considerable artistic challenges for them. I believe they are up to it, because of the kind
of noviceship that they have already served. So, not only is their immediate environment changing, but the circumstances in which their art will be received are changing radically.

In some organisations, this has given rise to a debate about selling out or becoming
part of the establishment. But it had always been the ambition of these organisations to have sufficient resources to do the job properly. You might say that the
Temple Bar initiative put it up to all of us who had been making these demands. It
was now time to put up or shut up.

*What is your response to the fears that have been expressed by arts practitioners
that Temple Bar's new cultural facilities will introduce sterility and formality into an
area that was characterised by the organic development of small-scale, independent arts organisations, and that there will be a sanitisation and loss of spontaneity?*

These are real dangers. I don't think that in any provision, particularly capital provision, you can guarantee that there will be quality, energy or relevance in work produced at a particular period. This phenomenon of the building working against the
production of vibrant art was a feature of the Abbey Theatre when it moved into its

*Model of the Photographic Centre,
now nearing completion on
Meeting House Square
(Group 91 / O'Donnell and
Tuomey Architects)*

55

present building in Marlborough Street. I remember theatre practitioners in the late sixties saying that what the Abbey needed then was another fire; they felt that the new building had stifled the aspirations of the national theatre. As that cycle ran its course, however, a more dynamic phase came around. It will take time for some organisations to stretch themselves to the capacity of their new facilities. There will be a dangerous tendency to go for what is possible rather than what is good. But if the organisations maintain a vibrancy within themselves, that can be overcome.

There was a feeling that the audience in Temple Bar was an alternative audience and that they might be turned off by having comfortable facilities. Certainly, many people using the facilities felt part of a movement of the dispossessed and felt that there was a political dimension to their involvement in the arts which they would now be robbed of. The content of the work will now need to have a sharper focus, and both artists and audiences may demand in it a stronger political dimension now that the ambience won't be reinforcing their alternative view of how society should be organised. The optimistic view, then, is that the new order in Temple Bar will strengthen the quality of the artistic statements made there in the long term.

Increasing access to the arts has been a stated priority of the Arts Council since the late seventies and early eighties. How do you think the Temple Bar initiative addresses the problem of vertical access? Isn't there a danger that this kind of culture-driven urban development benefits those who already enjoy a high level of economic and cultural capital?

This danger arises no matter where you engage in cultural development. All of the studies show a middle-class bias in terms of the audience profile for different art forms, although this varies of course, with film and popular music being perceived to be more egalitarian, less elitist. But there's a tendency for the words 'elitism' and 'quality' to become confused.

As our economy develops, the question of access to the arts is increasingly dictated by personal outlook, motivation and educational background, not by financial considerations *per se*. Price alone is not the turn-off, though this is not to be insensitive to the cost of accessing the arts, particularly the performing arts. People who work in the performing arts are so poorly paid that the question of admission prices is critical to their living standards. So you have to walk the line in your pricing policy between bringing in a return and not discouraging the public. But it's a question of marketing rather than social ideology, I think. A lot will depend on the management style too, as to how welcoming an arts facility is to a new audience.

That would apply in particular to the multi-media centre, Arthouse. Many people have no idea what it's all about.

Yes, that is probably the most challenging because of the

Before and after – studios in Temple Bar Gallery and Studios (McCullough Mulvin Architects)

Turnover and employment statistics from 'The Economic and Employment Impact of the Cultural Industries in Ireland' (1994)

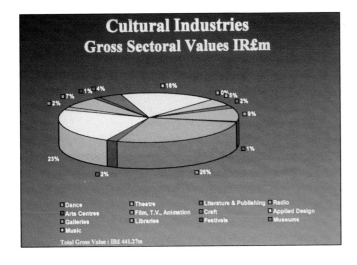

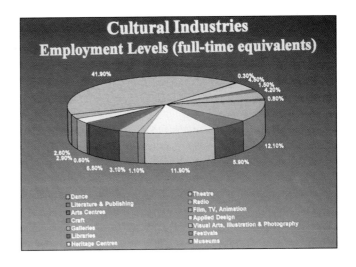

nature of it. It was driven by a desire to provide access to new media for artists who wanted to work outside the conventional forms. While my generation might have had an inferiority complex about establishing something like this, I think there's a new confidence in the generation that is coming up. They don't have to wait for somebody else to show them that something is a good idea.

These are the people who are managing the facilities in Temple Bar. The calibre of these arts administrators is the guarantee that the new, state-of-the-art facilities will not be sterile. They are in the hands of people who are aware of the issues and want to reach out to new audiences and young audiences. The general marketing image and hype that goes with Temple Bar, while being an encumbrance in some instances, will help new audiences to engage with the various cultural activities in the quarter.

To what extent does the Temple Bar project represent a departure from preceding cultural development strategies?

The Temple Bar project is an original, new and unfamiliar way of doing things, as it combines cultural development and urban renewal and is driven by the State rather than the private sector. This was a very imaginative departure in terms of public policy for urban development. It had not happened before and the concept was not easily won – it had to be fought for. There were significant pressures for the control of Temple Bar to pass into private hands.

The commitment to this cultural infrastructure marks the first coherent, planned provision of buildings for cultural purposes since the founding of the State. Prior to this, things happened in a one-off manner, for example, the National Concert Hall and two European City of Culture projects: IMMA and The Writers' Centre/Museum. Temple Bar was a flagship project in the European City of Culture year, and in any analysis of that particular cultural project, the very significant role of Lewis Clohessy, then director of the European City of Culture committee, must be acknowledged. He was the person who saw the opportunity to develop and resource this experiment in urban development.

Looking at urban renewal schemes around Europe, what is unique about Temple Bar is that the cultural dimension is organic. Development has been based on the number of small arts organisations already functioning in the area, so it is authentic. Rather than artificially inseminating the area with a cultural dimension, Temple Bar Properties has kept the integrity of what was already rooted there. It has been a bruising experience for the people involved, but they have managed to engage positively with the transition process.

Do you think it is a model that can be transferred to other urban centres and absorbed into future public policy?

Much of the philosophy that informed the Temple Bar development has been taken on board by the Arts Council and

articulated in the area-based strategy in the Arts Plan. The Cultural Development Incentive Scheme, run with EU funds under the National Plan, is also learning the lesson of a co-ordinated approach to planning. So the Temple Bar area has been a catalyst for infrastructural development around the country.

Temple Bar has also actively engaged in other cultural projects, such as holding conferences – for example, on the economy of the arts – and has commissioned research such as the Coopers and Lybrand report, bringing major institutional players together to examine the economic significance of the cultural industries. This is the context in which Temple Bar Properties views itself: acting as a think-tank and a catalyst in cultural debate, in issues of planning and developing relationships with other agencies, such as local authorities. For example, the location of the Temple Bar development, as an urban renewal scheme, in the Department of the Environment has had an enormously positive effect on how staff in that Department perceive the arts, because they have now engaged at first-hand with many of the issues.

In terms of public policy, there's an acknowledgement of the need to grow out of ad hoc cultural development. There was an attitude in the seventies, eighties and early nineties that too much planning would crush spontaneity. We have lived with the old 'poverty syndrome' – the institutional equivalent of the artist starving in the garret – which seemed to necessitate the existence of impossible obstacles in order to test the genuineness of the commitment of people working in the arts. I think as a society we are growing out of the syndrome that 'it will be all right on the night, we'll pull it off.' We've got that far; something more is needed now, and at least public policy is leading in this regard, not following.

This, of course, is creating controversy. Many people engaged in the arts are very sceptical and nervous about a growing State role in the arts, yet, looking at cultural infrastructure across Europe and in North and South America, it is clear that without the State taking an initiating role, the arts can only function in a market context. But the nature of much artistic endeavour means that it cannot be driven primarily by market forces.

What role do you envisage Temple Bar Properties will play in cultural activity in the future, as the whole area settles down?

Temple Bar Properties have been clear that there is first the building phase, which they have to manage and bring to completion, and then there will be the ongoing work and the relationship that they, as owners of these buildings, will have with the cultural organisations. That could be a rather difficult phase, not least because of the policy that Temple Bar Properties has introduced of having licences. The relationship between a licenser and licensee is not as secure as that between landlord and tenant, and the licence arrangement might be vulnerable to interference. In other words, dissatisfaction on the part of Temple Bar Properties (or its successor) with the activities of the arts organisations might lead to the impulse to interfere, to influence the quantity, quality, shape or direction of artistic work in the area. This would be wholly inappropriate and regressive. I'm not saying that any of the people involved have that kind of outlook or see that kind of future, but it is only by being aware of the danger that all parties involved will avoid these pitfalls.

Who is responsible in the long term for the ongoing subvention of these new cultural institutions?

Temple Bar Properties originated in the Department of the Taoiseach, which was also the mother department of the Arts Council. The early days were riddled with misunderstandings, misconceptions, rivalries and apprehensions about who was doing what and whether this new agency would inflict lasting damage to the primacy of the Arts Council's role in promoting artistic development and as a grant-aiding organisation. After a troublesome and difficult initial period, these two agents of the State have found a rationale. They have found that co-existence is not merely a truce, but that by dynamic interaction they can serve the general public policy and that it's not a question of one trying to usurp the other's function or territory. When both organisations were able to engage in constructive dialogue, there was an acceptance that there had to be a synergy between them, with Temple Bar Properties making it clear that in cases where they were providing buildings for organisations on the Arts Council's list, the Council had to be committed to the future of those organisations on the basis of the Council's own evaluation.

A feature of the early debate was, 'who will be responsible, who will pick up the tab', but in the longer run – and this is where the issue of licences mentioned earlier comes in – the question is: where will the ownership of the cultural institutions rest? Temple Bar Properties will probably be succeeded by a trust in the longer term. With the urban renewal project coming to completion, and since these are cultural institutions, their linkage with the Department of the Environment will become less relevant. As the Department of Arts, Culture and the Gaeltacht develops a constructive relationship with the Department of the Environment, it is reasonable to suppose that the structure that will be put in place will be arts-oriented, although this may evolve over a period of years.

The Arts Plan will be the principal influence on the arts environment in Ireland from now until the year 2000. The Arts Council has recognised the central importance of the Temple Bar Cultural Quarter in the plan, and it is the interaction between the cultural organisations and the Arts Council which will shape the success or otherwise of these organisations in the immediate future. The Council has set out in the plan the importance it attaches to strategic partnerships in promoting development in the arts sector. The Temple Bar experience has shown the dynamic which such partnerships can produce.

COLM Ó BRIAIN was the founding chairman of the Project Arts Centre. He is a former director of the Arts Council, and has worked in theatre, television and arts administration. He is currently Policy Advisor to the Minister for Arts, Culture and the Gaeltacht.

HELEN MEANY is a freelance journalist and writer.

Next in line – the redevelopment of the Project Arts Centre is currently at planning permission stage

Cities: Buildings and People

MATT McNULTY

I N THEMSELVES, CITIES ARE INTERESTING FOR TWO PREDOMINANT reasons. Firstly, they have been constructed incrementally over time, through a confluence of human vision and talent responding to the needs of government, commerce, religion and habitation. Secondly, being cities, their concentration can support the full expression of human endeavour in culture, art, sport, science, etc. These are the foundations for the attractiveness of cities. They thrive where the relationship between the physical and human elements are understood, enabled and enriched, through perceptive, integrated policies and the energy to effect them. They are diminished and weakened, conversely, through continued failure to repel attacks by urban diseases and infections which constantly assail them, or to heal injuries sustained.

The root energy which eventually blossomed and bore its fruit in the Temple Bar urban renewal project drew its strength and tenacity from many sources. Advocates of diverse interest groups saw merit in a large-scale, sensitive, integrated development of this key central area. It was made possible through the concentration of ownership in the hands of two public authorities: Dublin Corporation and CIÉ. It was made feasible through growing public and, therefore, political support, backed by the practical consideration of improving the city and the commercial consideration of supporting the tourism economy. Clearly, in the argument supporting the case, there was the self-evident potential for a strategic project of national scale, which could enhance the centre of Dublin, while preserving one of its most interesting and under-utilised and, for the public, most accessible areas.

The eventual case accepted by government was unique and untried in Ireland, in that it would be led not by commerce, but by tourism, culture and the arts, and so the birth of the concept of a 'cultural quarter' for Dublin took shape. To me, it was a concept I fully endorsed and advocated. I was, from the beginning, determined to be both a persuader and a supporter, as I saw considerable benefits, not only to the tourism economy of the city, but to conservation, culture and the arts. I was convinced, through my role in the Millennium, that the scale and potential of a renewed and reinvigorated Temple Bar would make an incisive contribution to the appearance, vibrancy and economy of Dublin. One of its determining strengths was that in tourism, cultural and arts terms, it gave practical expression to the technique of 'clustering', which understands and builds synergetically on many related elements.

With hindsight and the benefit of considerable achievement by the Temple Bar authorities, most commentators find themselves comfortably recognising its success. The project itself is recognised and lauded internationally as being at the leading edge of both urban renewal practice and thinking. The contribution the area has already made to the vibrancy and tourism economy of Dublin more than justifies our interest and support. The economic return is already clear, but the overall achievement goes much further.

The essence of its success for me is that the approach adopted was founded on a respect for historic and architectural elements. Within an overall leadership and integrated vision, it permitted diversity and imagination, and drew benefits from both. One of its ground-breaking achievements is that it brought purpose and progress to an area where there were a myriad of different agendas and divergent interests, and it did so within an empowering transparency and constant public debate which was welcomed and vigorously engaged in.

Cities, as I began with, are about the relationship of the physical aspects with people. One of the ultimate strengths of Temple Bar is that it restored the residential balance in the area and that it did so with the flair and panache which has, for me, characterised its overall success.

MATT McNULTY has been Director-General of Bord Fáilte since 1993 and has worked within the tourism industry for 30 years. In 1988 he was Managing Director of the Dublin Millennium, and he has served on many government-appointed boards, including Temple Bar Renewal Ltd, of which he is currently a director.

opposite – *Classical concert by the RTÉ Concert Orchestra, Parliament Street, 1994*

A private-sector perspective

JOHN F MULCAHY

FROM THE PRIVATE-SECTOR PERSPECTIVE, PERHAPS THE MOST REMARKABLE ASPECT OF the Temple Bar development is that it has happened. It has happened quickly and it has happened more or less exactly along the lines originally envisaged. Why is this remarkable? To appreciate that, it is first of all necessary to recognise the nature of the task that was being attempted. The objective was to harness private-sector investment in the pursuit of cultural and urban renewal objectives. The aim was to encourage the private sector to create what would be essentially a cultural rather than a commercial quarter. The State's contribution was to be mainly by way of tax incentives.

It would have been easy, five years ago, to dismiss this aspiration as impossible. (Indeed, many people did just that.) The history of urban renewal projects in Ireland would have suggested that maximising profit would have quickly become the overriding consideration affecting every development decision.

This would have brought about a profound difference between the scheme as originally envisaged and the scheme as actually developed. What was most profitable (in investment terms) would have been tackled first, followed after a possibly long interval by less profitable projects, and not followed at all by elements that the market found less attractive in profit terms than alternatives available elsewhere.

The cynic of five years ago, therefore, could reasonably have forecast that Temple Bar would develop very differently from the original plan, and also that it would

Temple Bar at Christmas time

opposite
The Cutlers, Parliament Street –
a mixed-use development of 23
apartments over retail ground floor

63

develop piecemeal over a much longer timescale than originally envisaged. What he could have expected to see by 1996 was the familiar sight of a half-developed project, lacking the synergy that can come only when all the pieces fall into place. Instead, what we are celebrating in 1996 is something not far short of a miracle in urban renewal terms. Before our eyes, the original vision for Temple Bar has taken shape. The timescale has been met. Dublin's cultural quarter is already a reality for all to see.

What are the lessons here for similar private sector/public sector projects? The main lesson, it seems to me, is that to harness market forces to non-market ends you must embark on a highly interventionist approach. It is not enough to lay a package of tax-incentives on the table and then expect the private sector to act out your chosen scenario. Without further intervention, the private sector will act out its own, purely profit-driven scenario – leaving any less commercial or non-commercial aspirations to quietly gather dust.

Temple Bar was particularly well-suited for an interventionist approach in that it started with the benefit of a large number of properties that were already in State hands. This benefit was consolidated by a sound legislative base that was in place from day one.

To carry out the actual interventionist policy, the focused task force approach used in Temple Bar appears to be an ideal vehicle. It's perhaps worth saying, however, that these mechanisms are only as good as the people involved. They are an enabling tool for entrepreneurial spirits, rather than a magic way of creating enterprise where none exists. For a successful renewal scheme of this kind, the calibre of the people involved will always be key. In addition to a feeling for enterprise, they need two other attributes that are not always found in great abundance in the public sector. One is the enthusiasm that fuels a determination to bite bullets where

bullets have to be bitten. A project of this kind will inevitably require the taking of decisions that don't please everybody. Fudge those decisions often enough and the original vision becomes diluted very quickly.

Equally necessary is a private-sector rather than a public-sector attitude towards time. One of the key realities of the market economy is that time is always of the essence, and nowhere more so than in a project of this type where the building of credibility to a critical mass is a key determinant of success or failure. Delaying decisions can be just as fatal as fudging them. All of these essential conditions have come together in Temple Bar. Decisions were neither fudged nor delayed, with the results we can see around us.

However, in celebrating the completion of the first phase, let us not forget that the task is far from finished. One of the remaining challenges will be establishing unquestionably the viability of retail activities. The success of the cultural and residential elements are not in doubt, but the retail dimension is perhaps going to take more time and ongoing management to get completely right.

This is not perhaps entirely unexpected, since patterns of shopping behaviour usually take a long time to shift. What is certain is that, given the success to date at Temple Bar, it would be a brave cynic indeed who would today forecast anything less than success for this dimension as well.

JOHN MULCAHY is Investment and Development Partner in Jones Lang Wootton. With JLW since 1970, he set up JLW Research, and takes a particular interest in innovations in the property marketplace. He graduated in Property Economics from the College of Technology, Bolton Street. He is a Fellow of the Royal Institution of Chartered Surveyors in Ireland, and an Associate of the Institute of Arbitrators.

The Joy of Coffee, Temple Bar

opposite

1	2
3	4

1 Spranger's Yard
  Fownes Street / Crow Street
2 5 Crow Street
3 Read's Cutlers, Parliament Street
4 DV8 Shoes, Crown Alley

Culture as innovative force

SERGIO ARZENI

A CCORDING TO SENATOR DANIEL PATRICK MOYNIHAN, THE CENTRAL CONSERVATIVE truth is that culture, not politics, determines the success of a society. The central liberal truth, he claims, is that politics can change culture and even save a culture from itself. Admittedly, the word 'culture' is vague and often used to refer to contradictory ideals, depending on political viewpoint and momentary convenience. It is only in focusing on the relationship between culture and progress that a definition of culture becomes possible.

Culture is a coherent system of values, attitudes and institutions that influence individual and social behaviour in all types of human experience. It moulds the territory in which people live, notably developing the uniquely human urban context. Urban culture fundamentally differs from rural culture in all countries. Peasants are individualistic, seeing themselves as threatened by their neighbours and their attempts at economic success. This outlook limits co-operative solutions and denies concepts of community welfare and social responsibility. Edward Banfield, in his seminal work *The Moral Basis of a Backward Society* analysed the social pathology of a rural area in southern Italy as being characterised by an inability to work together for a common, communitarian goal.[1]

Urban dwellers throughout history have shown an understanding of the value of the 'civic community', with its patterns of social co-operation based on tolerance, trust and norms of active citizen participation. These values thrived even in the Middle Ages in the communal republicanism of cities in central and northern Italy.

The new atrium in Temple Bar Gallery and Studios
(McCullough Mulvin Architects)

opposite
Rear façade of the Black Church Print Studio
(McCullough Mulvin Architects)

Robert Putnam argues that economic development does not explain political development.[2] Rather, ingrained patterns of civic community explain both a region's capacity for economic growth and also its capacity for democratic self-government. 'Civicness' and civic culture are vital as they open up an almost unlimited range of developmental possibilities. Putnam's argument implies – although he does not quite say so – that civicness is almost impossible to create where it does not already exist, as it is a function of time. However, while it is true that social capital is far harder to accumulate than physical capital, policies can play an important role in fostering or stymieing it nonetheless.

Urban renewal projects such as Temple Bar in Dublin have a value not only as means of restoring physical capital, but perhaps even more importantly in generating social capital based on creativity and communality. Investment in culture is paying off in Ireland, where a study by Coopers & Lybrand has recently shown that 'culture employs 33,800 people in the country (70% full-time) who are generating an output of 441 million punts out of which subsidies represent less than 12% of revenues'.

This highlights how the financial investment for the renaissance of Temple Bar is part of a more general strategy for Ireland to make culture a source of jobs and revenue, not just a pastime. The huge heritage of Wilde, Shaw, Joyce, Yeats, Synge, O'Casey or Beckett is an essential component of the Irish cultural industry, and Temple Bar has become its showcase. Europe recognised Dublin as a cultural capital of Europe, and Ireland eventually recognised the need to have a minister for culture. Would it have ever happened without Temple Bar? I doubt it, because of the economic and social impact of this project.

Francis Fukuyama argues very persuasively in his new book (*Trust: The Social Virtues and the Creation of Prosperity*, The Free Press, New York, 1995) that economic success only in part depends on traditional economic factors, such as markets, competition, technology and skills.[3] The kind of answers usually offered by economists in explaining success are only 80% right. The remaining 20% of a formula for economic success is explained by social capital. A supporting culture of trust or 'spontaneous sociability' which can be translated into a readiness to get on with one's fellow citizens in economically productive ways is key. In Fukuyama's words, 'Economic life is deeply embedded in social life, and cannot be understood apart from the customs, morals and habits of the society in which it occurs. In short, it cannot be divorced from culture.'

Is culture then equivalent to economic destiny? Fukuyama does not go so far. 'Culture is not an unbending, primordial force, but something shaped continuously by the flow of politics and history.' However, culture can be something more than this. As we have seen in discussing its impact on the urban scene, it can be the engine for economic, social and environmental transformation of the space in which we live.

Culture is not passive, rather it is one of the fastest growing and most labour-intensive industries in advanced nations. The expansion of leisure time and the growing demand for heritage, art, entertainment and cultural consumption are reshaping the function of cities and urban areas alike. Investments in art and aesthetic activities are viable and profitable in post-capitalist, knowledge-based economies.

The Pompidou Centre in Paris, with eight million visitors a year, is providing an excellent return on investment despite its extremely high maintenance costs. The Louvre Museum, after a capital investment which included the construction of the glass pyramid, has more than doubled its workforce from 2,500 to 6,000 by using its new facilities to add activities and initiatives to its core art exhibitions. The Netherlands has benefited enormously from hosting the Rembrandt exhibition in Amsterdam and Vermeer in Den Haag. This benefit is not just cultural but economic; the Dutch have developed a profitable international air charter business by bringing hundreds of thousands of people from all over the world to visit these two unique exhibitions.

Urban authorities can use culture as an innovative force in regenerating our cities and in creating jobs for the future. In doing so, however, they must understand that every attempt to rehabilitate historic sites, enhance the beauty of natural settings or find alternative roles for abandoned industrial plants faces the same challenge: how to balance the different interests represented in the urban environment in order to benefit and involve inhabitants.

To generate sustainable economic, social and cultural growth without damaging the environment beyond recall requires the management and preservation of the local heritage to count in local development plans. Surveys conducted by the Local Economic and Employment Development (LEED) Programme of the Organisation for Economic Cooperation and Development (OECD) in Paris have shown that successful attempts at this kind of sustainable growth have shared two common features: an integrated development strategy and a comprehensive partnership of all the involved actors.

In Europe, some cities began to revive when certain services such as the rehabilitation of old housing were taken in hand. This demand-based strategy both revitalised the need for skilled construction workers and at the same time improved the appearance and attraction of the city.

However, policy-makers should bear in mind a caveat to such thinking, proffered by Professor Leo Klaassen from Rotterdam:

'Tourism should be largely disregarded as a factor in the process of urban renewal, not because it is not worthwhile, but because in the hierarchy of values, it comes long after the requirements of a living local community which wants to be something else than just the keeper of a museum.'

Disregarding tourism is not being against tourism; it is just the contrary. When a historic town has been renovated according to sound ideas and principles, and has sought to provide for the local community, tourism will come anyway as a bonus. Tourism and local interests are far from opposed in the sphere of urban regeneration.

The example of Temple Bar is a case in point. In a country largely relying on rural tourism, the creation of such a 'culture hub' in the inner city of Dublin, so close to the mythical Trinity College, has transformed the function of the city on tourists' maps. Dublin has become a real destination for cultural tourism in Europe. Even more unbelievable for a country of emigration, Temple Bar and the fiscal facilities available there have made Dublin a destination sought after by European artists and intellectuals looking for a pleasant cultural environment in which to live.

In its recent participation in the Milan Triennale, the LEED programme sought to demonstrate the complementary nature of economic, aesthetic and social consideration in public policy by showcasing a number of notable success stories. In Antwerp, different levels of government have worked together to use a beautiful old building not only as a modern railway station, but also as a cultural centre and as the offices for a local small business scheme. Temple Bar in Dublin has capitalised on an existing core of artistic ventures to renew an old and historic area of the city, bringing in new long-term jobs and adding to the city's cultural life. The other examples in Italy and France also seek to promote economic and cultural regeneration in urban areas through a multi-dimensional, multi-actor approach.

In highlighting these policy successes, the LEED programme is not trying to suggest that policy has overcome the essential component of 'civicness' and culture in economic success; rather it is emphasising the importance of exploiting and developing cultural factors in parallel with economically targeted programmes. It offers not a solution of culture as opposed to economics and politics; instead it seeks to show that these are all concepts that are inextricably intertwined and which must be treated in the light of this reality.

References

[1] Edward Banfield, *The Moral Basis of a Backward Society* (The Free Press, New York, 1958)
[2] Robert Putnam, *Making Democracy Work: Civic Traditions in Modern Italy* (Princeton University Press, 1993)
[3] Francis Fukuyama, *Trust: The Social Virtues and the Creation of Prosperity* (The Free Press, New York, 1995)

SERGIO ARZENI is an economist. He is currently the head of the Local Economics and Employment Development Programme (LEED) at the Organisation for Economic Co-operation and Development (OECD) in Paris.

The arched entrance of the National Photographic Archive (Group 91 / O'Donnell and Tuomey Architects)

The Public Art Programme

AIDAN DUNNE

W HEN SCULPTOR AND ARCHITECT FILIPPO BRUNELLESCHI WON A PUBLIC COMPETI-
tion in 1432 for the right to design the crowning stage of the massive
dome for Florence Cathedral, the technically demanding project
marked the vaunting self-confidence of the Italian city-states. The city-
states that had their origins in the eleventh century are worlds away from contemporary nation-states. But Brunelleschi and his contemporaries were not only engaged
in making the most public art imaginable, commissioned and overseen by representative councils drawn from the guilds, they were also in the process of creating
the very notion of painters, sculptors, architects with which we are still familiar
today. Those practices were not, at the time, counted among the seven liberal arts,
and were tagged onto vaguely appropriate categories in the complex system of
guilds. That they quickly became discrete and extremely prestigious activities is a
reflection not of arbitrary policy but of their inescapable relevance at the time.

We have moved from a situation in which architectural design and the practice of
the fine arts were becoming increasingly central to the fabric of the state in which
they flourished, to one in which artists and architects face rather different constraints and priorities. Art has lost its centrality, its perceived pivotal role in defining
cultural identity. Instead, a cynic might say, we have the Percent for Art scheme run
by the Department of the Environment. As architect Angela Rolfe, intimately
involved in the issues of contemporary public art, put it at a conference organised
by the Sculptors' Society of Ireland in 1995: 'In the past, society and its leaders
demanded that architects and artists work together because their work was valued

Darrel Viner
In Sight, *1995*
Temple Bar Gallery and Studios
lights, electrical circuits

opposite
James Scanlon
Under a Low Sun, *1996*
The Ark
mild steel, patinated copper, etched flashed
glass, plasterboard, 15.2 x 3.4m

by the public ... A mandatory 1% label betrays the bad conscience of a society trying to tack on a bit of culture rather late in the day ... Does society value art and architecture?'

The bad conscience extends beyond the bounds of the Percent for Art scheme to architecture itself. Temple Bar is a rare example of architects being given the freedom to actively create a language of form and function as they design rather than, in a climate of wariness and caution, infill with pastiche façades. There is the salutary example just over the river on Bachelor's Walk of a vast development which represents the false virtue of conservation at all costs.

However it is judged in the longer term, and whatever the long-term viability of the cultural institutions that form such an essential part of it, Temple Bar provides the best working example we have seen to date, in Dublin, of a creative collaboration between artists and architects. It has opened a window of opportunity which both have been quick to exploit, and their efforts can, at least, be judged on their merits rather than in terms of outside constraints within which they might otherwise have had to operate.

The equivalent, in public art terms, of cod-Georgian buildings would be cod-Imperial monuments. Such monuments, Imperial or otherwise, correspond to the narrowest conception of public art: an art of the State, by the State and for the State, putting its permanent stamp of ownership and authority on its communal spaces. In Ireland we have witnessed a logical progression in such public art. The symbols of colonial power and authority coexisted with and eventually ceded to nationalist dominance. Oliver Sheppard's statue of Cuchulainn in the GPO, or his figures commemorating the 1798 Rising in Wexford, Augustus St Gauden's Parnell monument in O'Connell Street, all typically celebrate and monumentalise a national identity in terms of history and myth, but it can be argued that they borrow their sculptural language from the colonial power.

More recently, sculptors like Edward Delaney and John Behan also set out to embody an essentially Celtic cultural identity, drawing on myth and literature in their public projects. The difference is, perhaps, that they approached the task in terms of a personal vernacular. Other major projects like Edwin Lutyens' memorial park at Islandbridge for those slain in the First World War, or Jerome Connor's Lusitania monument, found their nationalistic counterpart in the Garden of Remembrance in Parnell Square.

With the rise of Modernist architecture, Dublin, as much as any sizeable city in Europe and the US, saw the advent of the plaza sculpture. There are two basic forms: the organic, Henry Moore-like, and the geometric, David Smith-like. The works embellish the landscaped forecourts created by designers of high-rise office blocks. Detractors point out that they reflect the corporate blandness of multi-national culture, and while corporate artworks may be public, they usually turn their backs on the interests of the viewer.

The crises in urban planning have been echoed in the realm of public art, and the last two decades have witnessed a radical and continuing process of reassessment. The process has been instrumental in bringing about the implementation of the Percent for Art scheme, which, it must be emphasised, has, despite its shortcomings, been a positive development, energetically and creatively employed by Cork's Niall Hegarty for one. The pending review of the Percent scheme, undertaken by a committee of government departments and agencies and chaired by the Department of the Environment, in fact arose as a result of a proposal from Temple Bar Properties, based on their experience of commissioning public art in the context of a major urban renewal project.

Such contemporary sculptors as Richard Long, Chris Drury and David Nash not only site their work in the natural environment in various ways, outside of a conventional commercial or museum context, they also exemplify growing sensitivity to that environment. Unsurprisingly, this coincides with the growth of sculpture parks, particularly in Scandinavian countries, and evidenced here in the regional Sculpture Trails, such as those in Co Sligo or north Mayo. There have been urban developments as well, such as Dublin's Sculpture Trail. Limerick's annual exhibition, EV⁺A, in 1994 and 1996 made ambitious and, on the whole, successful attempts to bring art from the museum context into the city's communal spaces.

All this serves to underline that public art is not a straightforward term and is dogged by questions of definition. Many shades of meaning can be read into the word public – State, communal, populist, social. An abiding problem is that virtually all art is to some extent public. In fact, the epithet public might have more to do with an artwork's concerns than with its siting, so that it may legitimately be argued that any particular museum work is more public than a repressive but publicly sited monument.

This question of definition is particularly significant in relation to Temple Bar in the light of the number of working cultural institutions that have been established within its precincts. These institutions are in various explicit and implicit ways integral to any consideration of public art in the context of Temple Bar. That is to say, the institutions represent a tangible commitment to process. Public art cannot be simply a matter of imposing a number of static, permanent artworks in a given geographical area. The institutions have a public presence and also a public function. In this respect, the unproven nature of some of them – Arthouse, The Ark – is actually all the more exciting.

Outside of this, what Temple Bar Properties itself specified as its public art programme falls into three categories. The first is the series of annual street art projects. These were, by definition, temporary events, effected while the area was in the throes of dramatic change, challenging artists with an environment that was drastically disrupted. It is notable that so many artists devised strategies that engaged critically with

Grace Weir
Untitled, *1996*
Dublin's Viking Adventure
glass-reinforced fibre with bronze insets

John Kindness
Teething troubles in an energy-
efficient restaurant, *1995*
ESB sub-station, Crow Street
steel frame, enamelled steel plates
2.4 x 2.2 m

Maud Cotter
Absolute Jellies Make Singing Sounds
Green Building, Temple Lane, 1994
copper, brass, lead, aluminium, glass,
perspex, 6 x 2.5 m

Róisín de Buitléar
Untitled, *1996*
DIT School of Photography
glass, steel cladding, 40cm x 350cm x 30cm

the physical surroundings and with the wider issues of what was happening to Temple Bar. Many pieces manifested an ambivalence about the nature and pace of development; others were more positive, but, in general, few chose to ignore what was going on. They also, however, showed a lively interest in the question of what public art might be.

As part of the first street art exhibition, curated by Artsource in 1992, Paki Smith and Ronan Halpin's *The Wounded King* was a *coup de theatre* and an interesting piece of public sculpture. A nude male figure, it was monumental in scale while belying the conventions of monumentality in that it was temporary, highly portable, very colourful, and made of lightweight materials. Its Arthurian reference was apposite for Temple Bar. Eoin Byrne's optimistic *Something From Nothing* offered a time-lapse succession of images of a flower blooming, ingeniously arranged against the ready-made grid of a brick building. By the time building work was in full swing the following year, the area was a maze of hoardings, and artists were offered these as ready-made canvases, inviting a number of impressive responses.

Paul O'Reilly took up residence and drew, with a brush, a series of portraits, temporarily recording likenesses of whoever passed by. In a similar vein, Peter Jones collaborated with Aideen Lynch to produce a polished series of hand shadow images. Corban Walker sited tinted windows at various heights (he had in mind assumptions about appropriate heights), looking onto the drama of a building site. Clea van der Grijn's distorting reflective surfaces offered a wry comment on the area's metamorphosis. Similarly, Lisa Harmey made giant puncture repair patches that strained to hold together the sides of the infill sites. What these works have in common is a quality of engagement with the immediate human experience of Temple Bar, with the work in progress, and with the underlying issues, the debate extant about the relative merits of the area's radical shift in identity.

The second category encompasses what might be termed some of Temple Bar Properties' showcase buildings. These include the cultural centres, the Green Building and No.5 Crow Street. Practically every project entailed the close collaboration of artists and architects. Most of them are on a major scale, like Grace Weir's wall relief for Dublin's Viking Adventure, which offers a visualisation of the site's history, a conceptual snapshot encompassing navigational maps, a Viking longboat, castings taken from Viking artefacts and other pertinent details.

The Green Building blurs the edge between art and architecture. Its art elements, in which the dominant metaphor is recycling, have a functional component and are stitched seamlessly into the fabric of the building, from James Garner's recycled copper boilers which clad the exterior pillars, to the doors and frames by Maud Cotter and Remco de Fouw (both exhibit a sense of humour), to Brian McDonald's recycled TV screen lights and signs, and Vivienne Roche's canvas duct in the atrium.

In the Music Centre on Curved Street, Gerard Byrne pursues a dialogue with the building's structural grammar, and prompts the occupants and visitors to do likewise by making windows onto the blocks, joists, pipes and conduits beneath the plastered, finished surfaces, exposing the functional armature. Daryl Viner's pavement-set lights outside Temple Bar Studios create a visible link between the street and the building. Running water and other utilities inside the building control the switches which turn the lights on outside.

Elsewhere, artists buckled down cheerfully to functional roles, as in the magnificent gates to Designyard – recognisable versions of her drawings based on city maps and anatomical details – by Kathy Prendergast (working with blacksmith Harry Page), the Black Church Print Studio's doors by Andrew Folan, Mirjam Keune's fireplace, and James Scanlon's stained glass installations for The Ark, including both the basement installation and the windows fronting Meeting House Square. Again, significantly, rather than the imposition of an autonomous aesthetic scheme, there is a critical engagement with the nature of each space, its uses and meanings for the individuals who pass through it.

Felim Egan also mediates between Eustace Street and Meeting House Square in a work that extends, with lights, through the linking tunnel, and culminates in what is really a sculptural version of one of his paintings on a grand scale, using lead as a ground colour. It is not only a fine work in its own right, but a triumph of architectural design as well.

The third category encompasses art for public spaces. Although it is probably what most people would think of first in relation to public art, it is but one strand among many. In this sense of the term, the most ambitious public art scheme yet mooted in Ireland was Christo's as yet unfulfilled proposal to cover the paths in St Stephen's Green. In Temple Bar it includes such street furniture as Betty Maguire's annotated *Historic Seat*, and Rachel Joynt's film reel motif at the entrance to the Irish Film Centre. The Christmas tree in Temple Bar Square also comes into this category, and it is not to diminish the individual achievements within it to say that the extent and nature of the whole gamut of projects in the quarter demonstrate how narrow a category it is in itself.

Ultimately the strength of the Public Art Programme in Temple Bar lies in the extent to which it harks back to that unified view of joint endeavour described by Angela Rolfe and exemplified in the Florentine city-state. Public relevance is integral to this process. Projects like the development of Temple Bar – and no others currently spring to mind – are the way we will find out whether public art has a future, something that is not a foregone conclusion either way.

AIDAN DUNNE is art critic for the *Sunday Tribune*. He is also the author of many books and catalogues on Irish art and artists.

We need walls
and we don't need walls

AN ARTIST'S PERSPECTIVE

MARTINA GALVIN

M
Y MEMORIES OF TEMPLE BAR GO BACK TO WHEN I WAS A FINE ART STUDENT AT
NCAD in the 1980s. I was drawn to gallery openings, public lectures and
debates at the Project Arts Centre and Temple Bar Gallery and Studios.
This was an essential part of college life. I also remember going to the
Bad Ass Café, the Norseman, the music recording studios and the bicycle shop.
The small streets had and still have a sense of intimacy, and you knew that you
were in a creative environment. I left Dublin in 1988 to live in Wicklow for one year,
and then moved on to Cardiff. I came back to Dublin in 1994, to the euphoria of the
ceasefires in Northern Ireland, looking for studio space, and eager to immerse
myself in the exciting cultural activities that were happening in Dublin.

The atmosphere was pumping with vitality and life, especially the Temple Bar area,
which had undergone dramatic alterations since the 1980s, physically and culturally. The debate is different now. The agenda includes the rights of artists, cultural
politics, tax incentives, commerce and status. New kinds of art practices are facilitated. Artists can engage in and explore new media and new technologies. Temple
Bar seemed to be the centre of activity and attention, although not the only new
centre for art activity in the city. The clustering together of the different creative centres, some old, some new, alongside the huge number of restaurants and coffee
shops, creates the potential for a dynamic creative environment.

Studio space was hard to find, as it is in any city, especially on a long-term basis. I
worked at the Fire Station Artists' Studios in Buckingham Street for three months.

Late-night art in Temple Bar

opposite
Ronan Halpin and Paki Smith's
Wounded King visited Temple Bar as
part of Temple Bar Street Art 1992

77

There I meet up with three artists on a similar search for a studio, and we have now formed a studio group on Foley Street, where we signed a five-year lease. In the intervening period, I worked in Temple Bar Gallery and Studios. It was the summer of 1995 and I was working on a commission for the Bank of Ireland, which resulted from a group exhibition at the Fire Station Artists' Studios.

The experience of working in the project studio in Temple Bar Gallery was exciting and rewarding. The studio space provided what I considered to be the right conditions for creating work – good light, heat and privacy, the extremely helpful and supportive staff, and enthusiastic artists. For me, these conditions made working there very productive. The international studio and the project studio facility offer an important extension to the activities of the Temple Bar Studios, in that artists from outside the area, or even outside the country may come, to work in Temple Bar, engaging with the artists there and continuing on a dialogue that started when the building was first occupied by Brian Maguire, Patrick Graham, Robert Armstrong, Joe Hanly and Jenny Haughton.

The most important and significant aspect of the development of Temple Bar Gallery and Studios is that the artists who work there are provided with professional working spaces adequate to their needs, and they have control in decision-making and the running of the building. They also have access to opportunities for the exposure of their work, and support structures to facilitate their other professional needs. A secure working environment has been created and will be maintained for artists. It took an enormous amount of time and effort on the part of all those involved to create this situation, and I felt it was a privilege as an artist returning to Dublin to be offered the facilities of the project studio.

In Cardiff I spent two years doing an MA in Fine Art. I was the only painter on the course and this provided for engaging and challenging debates with students and tutors alike. I came back to Dublin with an open view on the interaction between different disciplines and a clearer understanding of the importance of this in my work, and other artists' work.

Temple Bar offers the possibility and opportunity for interaction between creative disciplines, through the facilities in the area. There is a need for these facilities to be available to artists as tools for the expression of ideas. They will allow Irish artists to be au fait with new technology, and to handle their chosen medium with competence. I see Temple Bar as an incredibly rich resource for artists, and a facility that, if used to its fullest potential, will facilitate exciting and innovative work from artists. For those involved in film, editing, photography, print-making, music, sound recording, performance, video and interactive media work, equipment is available to facilitate the artist's needs in these areas. Training courses and programmes are available at different levels.

In February 1996, I participated in a group show, a joint initiative of The Ark and Temple Bar Gallery. The Ark had an exhibition of poems, drawings and paintings made by children from the Terezin Ghetto near Prague while incarcerated in a concentration camp during the Second World War. In Temple Bar Gallery, eight artists responded to this work, while in The Ark there were workshops for children. I welcomed the opportunity to participate in this show, especially as I had visited Auschwitz and Birkenau while in Poland.

Over the past fourteen months I have been involved in a number of projects and exhibitions abroad with the Artists Museum, which have been particularly inspiring. The Artists Museum, established in Poland in 1981, can best be described as a museum without walls. It is an artist-run group which organises large gatherings of artists at certain geographical and temporary points, to generate a transitory, creative turbulence of energy. In April 1995, I was invited to participate in 'The Fifth Construction in Process', which was a two-week gathering of 100 artists from twenty different countries, in a town in the Negev desert in Israel. I also participated in Artists Museum events in Wales, Finland and Germany, and was invited to exhibit in the Artist's Museum Gallery in Lodz in Poland. Being involved with this group has been a powerful and moving experience, and has influenced my ideas about the process of making art, the relevance of the art object from an Eastern European perspective, and the responsibilities of artists.

The international exchange of cultural, political and artistic ideas has been inspirational, and has given me a broader understanding of art and artists' lives in these countries. The cultural, national and social context within which we all work is varied, but there is one common thread – the belief that artistic activity could, did and will cross these boundaries and barriers. Artistic activity meaning not solely the creation of art objects, but the activity of being an artist, expressing freely thought and emotions. It is particularly poignant for those artists who, in the past, have worked in countries where being active as an artist could and did land you in prison. It put my own working environment in perspective.

This experience has also put into perspective for me, as an artist, what is the most essential and vibrant aspect of Dublin city and the cultural development programmes that have taken place over the past few years. The exchange of ideas and opinions between creative people, as well as the work that they make, is an essential and vital part of Temple Bar. Care has to be taken to ensure that this is not submerged by commerce and tourism. This aspect of the cultural development programme needs to be given as much attention as the walls that are built around the artists to protect them, for as artists, we need walls and we don't need walls.

MARTINA GALVIN, a Dublin-based visual artist, has exhibited in Ireland, Wales, England, Finland, Poland and Israel. Later in 1996 she will exhibit at Temple Bar Gallery, Dublin, and in Cologne.

Temple Bar Gallery and
Studios (above) and Artists at work in
the new studios in Black Church Print
Studio (below)

The city takes shape

ROBERT MAXWELL

I T IS FIVE YEARS SINCE TEMPLE BAR PROPERTIES ORGANISED A competition to find ways of restructuring the Temple Bar area. The competition produced twelve interesting entries drawn from large and small architectural studios, and it is perhaps a happy augury that it was won by a group of young architects who had combined under the name of Group 91 Architects. These young architects, by their joint approach to the framework plan, created the conditions for a result that would reflect not only a common purpose, but a varied response. They were all hungry to design buildings and young enough to seize any chance, but they shared a vision of the thoroughly modern architecture that would refresh Irish eyes and still generate the elements of traditional city form.

Five years on, the benefits of their accord are plain to see. The area is developing consistently and logically, but without the excessive design control that has spoiled so many recent attempts at moulding civic space. Each studio has worked to demonstrate its excellence in designing buildings, but never at the expense of taking over the common ground. The personal differences in their approaches have contributed to a lively and assorted mixture that blends easily into the street, even if it proclaims its own certainty. There is nothing 'themed' about the result. The area retains its original character as a grid of small streets, mixing historic relics and commercial accidents, and the new insertions have not compromised its character or harmed its vitality. In promoting the competition and in trusting in its outcome, the Government has shown something like wisdom, and this is enough to make the result unusual as well as impressive. Much remains to be done. There are still unwanted spaces and decrepit remains, but it is not premature to declare a success in the making.

For the overseas critic, there is a special interest in the initiative because it seems to mark a moment in the development of Irish culture that benefits from a horizon that is plainly European rather than Anglo-Saxon. The holding of the competition coincided with the year of Dublin's designation as European City of Culture. In the very concept of proposing new buildings that at the same time define public spaces, the critic can discern a debt to certain broad ideas about continuity in the city that stem from the Italian Aldo Rossi and the Luxembourgeois Léon Krier. European cities on the whole have been more aware of their inherited context than the New World cities, with their lust for skyscrapers and their duty to fill the void. Krier worked for a time with the English architect James Stirling, and several of the members of Group 91 learned their craft in Stirling's office. Stirling himself had a vision of a modern architecture that would never be compromised by half measures, yet would be capable of working with the existing context. Stirling was undoubtedly influenced by the architectural critic Colin Rowe, who used his observations of Italian cities – particularly Rome – to criticise the ideological nature of technological modernism, obsessed by the single building and oblivious to the city as a whole. To these influences we can perhaps add a Spanish dimension, since David Mackay, a key member of the competition assessors, practises in Spain. The vitality of recent Spanish architecture, after the removal of Fascist constraints, has been compelling, and the way in which the city of Barcelona in particular has benefited from its role as venue for the 1992 Olympic Games has been exemplary and exhilarating. The year 1991 was a good year for Dublin, when it achieved the status of a truly European city.

Dublin as a city is luckier than most in the very fact that it has not been eviscerated by high-rise monsters. There are a few regrettable instances, it is true, but the city still holds together, with its Georgian and Victorian inheritance, its superb set-pieces, and the peculiar scale and modest size that allowed Joyce to underpin *Ulysses* with Bloom's peripatetic philosophising across its width and breadth. It is a city that has been written about, that is impregnated with its tragic history and that resonates with the literary amplification of its events. How satisfactory then that it should now be able to demonstrate that history does not kill development, that the endemic conditions of post-Modernism are not a cause for despair.

The result must depend a great deal on the policy by which Temple Bar Properties has been partly funded by the State, but given the freedom to raise private funding as well, and to pursue its aims of cultural regeneration without undue interference. A system of tax incentives has been approved, and this gives a means of drawing in new sponsors, who expect to be able to operate eventually on a fully competitive commercial basis. This initiative allows the whole venture to cut years off the normal period of waiting for values to rise. At the same time, to be able to count on government support in setting up the new cultural centres has been a great advantage. And for the young architects, to be able to design for modest institutions as well as for those ventures that are immediately viable commercially has been opportunity and challenge combined.

So we have a film centre, a photographic archive, a multimedia centre, a music centre – for pop as well as classical music – an applied arts centre, a children's centre, a Viking exhibition centre. None of these is a free-standing building; all of them are attached at some point to the existing city fabric. In all of these cases, the designers have taken seriously the implications of building not just *in* but *into* the city.

An important feature of the Group 91 framework plan was the policy of accommodation to the scale and texture of the existing city fabric. This from the beginning meant more than observing frontages and height limitations. It involved paying attention to the way buildings address and clarify existing spaces, and also mould the spaces behind them, where back land has the potential to open up to new pedestrian ways. In addition, there has been a will to make new spaces appropriate to the quarter: an entirely new street joining two adjacent streets, to improve east-west permeability, for example; and, more conspicuously, the transformation of empty sites previously used as car-parks to create new squares.

In the case of Temple Bar Square, a new mixed-use and residential development looks north across the whole south side of the square, defining it as an enlargement of Temple Bar – the main east-west route – and incidentally creating a sort of skateboard forum, a place for junior to hang out, for mothers to gossip. In the case of Meeting House Square, all four sides of a new place have been defined by new buildings – by different hands, all different. An auditorium opens into this space for open-air performances, and films will be projected from one side of the space to the other. It is more of a room than a street. This amounts to a revitalisation of the actual city square as opposed to the ritual 'open space' incorporated into a single building entity – the result of 'comprehensive redevelopment' – in faint-hearted imitation of the traditional square.

There are two aspects of this development that provoke some astonishment: the evenhandedness that allows the State to intervene without dictating every detail, leaving the development open to market opportunities without renouncing a central interest in preserving community values; and the fact that there appears to be a complete absence of ideological fervour – the sort of either/or sectarianism that in London has produced a stiff confrontation between overly modern high-tech and over-reactionary Classical Revival.

There is one aspect of all this that is especially unusual to the eyes of the architectural critic: the variety of the architectural interventions, some of which blend into the street architecture by their judicious use of brickwork, others of which stand out by their international whiteness and uncompromising newness. Cities are sites for the mutual definition of order and variety. At the level of the architects' persuasion and personal preferences, how has this marvellous combination of order and variety come about?

Perhaps it was in the coherence of a group of like-minded people who had the wit to club together to present a joint programme for a big project. If this is the case, we are better off than if the competition had been won by a single large office, in which case the variety would have been largely simulated or produced by design management, but these buildings are genuinely varied, in style as well as in formation. One is reminded of the strange case of the Festival of Britain,

above – *Meeting House Square*
(drawing by Rachel Chidlow)

below – *Temple Bar Framework Plan, 1991*

pages 80-81
Meeting House Square, set up for a film screening,
June 1996

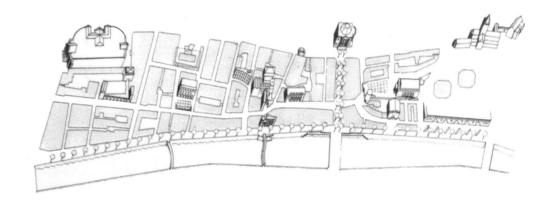

when Hugh Casson masterminded a conglomerate of architects and had them co-operate to create the South Bank Exhibition, full of picturesque juxtaposition in the manner of the artist Gordon Cullen. At the time, young architects like myself, who were scornful of the very idea of managing variety, characterised the result as kitsch. Years later, Reyner Banham was able to show that a remarkable unity underlay that variety, perhaps simply the unity of the moment that was 1951. There seems to be a unity underlying the variety of the Temple Bar interventions. Perhaps it lies in a particular moment, the moment of the advent of the European horizon (inseparable from the moment of incurring excessive success in the Eurovision Song Contest). Perhaps it is a moment when modern architecture is finally absorbing the lessons of post-Modernism, the realisation that all solutions are conditional, not absolute, that art – including architecture as art – is borne on the back of an invisible elephant, itself carried along on the back of an invisible tortoise, swimming in a sunless sea (an Indian myth on the nature of the cosmos, approximating to the Barthesean idea of Culture as Container). Or it may be less momentous, a transitory pulse in the tide of fashion.

Certainly, there is a preponderance in these buildings of modern functional planning, the residue of a Corbusian aesthetic that combines largely orthogonal room layout with the judicious use of curves at points of emphasis – some really neat planning. There are large windows, but the areas of plate glass stop short of being window walls. The principal elevations show combinations of openings of different sizes, rather than being made up of uniform repetitions. Buildings are sometimes broken into different parts and differentiated by the use of different materials. Internally, there is a flow of modern space, around corners and up through different

floors, but with a judicious use of separation and of separate rooms when appropriate. There is a lot of reinforced concrete, civilised by the application of stucco. And almost all the window frames, staircases and elevator cages are in welded steel, which imparts a tough-mindedness along with the conversational flow.

Difficult for the critic to differentiate between so much excellence. I am particularly impressed by the resourcefulness of Shay Cleary Architects (Arthouse – the multi-media centre) on Curved Street; by an agile lightness of touch in the work of Derek Tynan (the Printworks – a mixed-use and residential building on East Essex Street); by the sense of archetype always dramatically present in the work of O'Donnell and Tuomey (the Irish Film Centre and the Photographic Centre). These are personal preferences, but every building I saw on a recent tour had something original and suggestive to offer.

It is quite remarkable that this feast of modern, useful and stylish buildings should come hand in hand with such care and even love for the pre-existing architecture of the city. Shay Cleary's multi-media centre incorporates an old house, preserving enough to speak for it without inhibiting the new spaces with which it communicates – an exercise in sheer tact. Shane O'Toole's and Michael Kelly's children's centre on Eustace Street retains the complete street frontage of the old Presbyterian Meeting House, and insinuates behind it an extraordinary universe of Jack-and-the-Beanstalk marvels, scaled to the world of a child. One of these marvels is the way the auditorium is transformed into a summer proscenium; the backcloth screen rises up to form an outward projecting canopy, and the building reveals to Meeting House Square its alter ego – modern architecture with a human face.

Arthouse (Group 91 / Shay Cleary Architects)

The Printworks (Group 91 / Derek Tynan Architects)

None of these buildings-in-the-city has compromised itself by a sentimental front or a dilution of its own convictions. Grafton Architects' south side to Temple Bar Square does not impose a classical ideal, but follows out an inner compulsion to explore asymmetry and abstracted balance. It nonetheless responds to its duty to provide the frontage that establishes a new square in the public realm. The mixture of public duty and private indulgence is somehow a mark of candour, a gauge of genuine feeling in a situation where many interests are at stake.

One is completely bemused by the sensitive way Austin Dunphy has preserved and restored an old 1733 house in Eustace Street, not ideologically committed to a doctrinaire and mythical ideal, but allowing the character of successive periods to appear as one progresses upward through the floors – a compromise that does not cheat history. Or one is agreeably diverted by Seán O'Laoire's Green Building, an experiment in environmental reconciliation that is also a stylish essay in street architecture on both its east and west façades.

Perhaps the clue to the overall success of these young architects lies in an earlier essay by Group 91, the polemical proposal contained in the exhibition titled *Making a Modern Street*, which established at a theoretical level the principles that underlie the concrete results obtained in Temple Bar. Modern voices add up to a traditional form. The result echoes, in a curious way, the Rue Mallet-Stevens in Paris, where a group of diverse avant-garde architects in the twenties succeeded in having some modern villas constructed, not in the ideal modernist park, but in a street – the destination of 99% of all taxi rides, the street that participates in the aggregate system of streets that we call the city.

Across the river from Temple Bar, a large development has just been completed under an entirely different system. The old Dublin is recaptured, not in spirit, but in appearance. Along Bachelor's Walk, the scale and plot divisions of the old quay have been restored by design management so that, from across the river, the past seems to have been retrieved. On closer inspection, this is the result of imitation, of the space of appearance. The result was foreseen, foreordained. In Temple Bar, a different method has led to more interesting and more genuine results. The life of the city has been extended by renewing the system that gave rise to it in the first place. It's not the last word; it's an ongoing show that commands our respect.

Is the result Irish? Not in any obvious way, but all the same, it has a native quality – in the small scale and the unpretentiousness, in its improvisatory nature, in a certain quick-wittedness and conversational aplomb. It is certainly agreeable in the way that Dublin has always seemed agreeable – not overwhelming, not monothematic, but open-ended, personable, and, incidentally, providing the material for a literary narrative. It provides a salutary lesson to government and people alike.

ROBERT MAXWELL is an architect and critic, and has written extensively about architectural and urban issues. He was Professor of Architecture at University College London from 1979 to 1982, and Dean of the School of Architecture at Princeton University from 1982 to 1989. He now lives and works in London, and lectures at the Architectural Association and elsewhere. His most recent publication is *Sweet Disorder and the Carefully Careless – Theory and Criticism in Architecture* (Princeton, 1993).

Photographic Centre (Group 91 / O'Donnell and Tuomey)

The Ark (Group 91 / Shane O'Toole and Michael Kelly)

Urban Design

INTRODUCTION

THE DEVELOPMENT PROGRAMME FOR TEMPLE BAR IS MORE than a series of individual cultural, residential and commercial projects, however compelling or worthwhile these may be in their own right. All of these projects have been undertaken by Temple Bar Properties within the flexible framework of an overall urban scheme. The urban framework plan for Temple Bar emerged as the result of a competition held in 1991, for which twelve architectural practices entered proposals. These were considered by a team of assessors which included an independent external specialist (David Mackay, who has contributed an essay to this book), as well as representatives of Dublin Corporation Planning Department, the RIAI (the representative body for architects in Ireland), and Temple Bar Properties (the client).

Group 91 Architects, a combined practice of eight small architectural practices were the winners of this competition, and their urban scheme was published and exhibited by Temple Bar Properties under the title *Temple Bar Lives* in 1991.

A large part of that plan has now been implemented, including residential and commercial developments throughout the entire area, all but one of the twelve cultural projects, and the making of two new squares and the new street.

This section sets out the original principles of the urban framework plan for Temple Bar, and revisits them in the light of what has actually been done in the intervening period of five years.

A second phase, including Project Arts Centre / Crampton Court and the remaining undeveloped area west of Parliament Street, will begin in 1996.

PQ

Urban Design

The Framework Plan

ORIGINS AND UPDATE

JOHN TUOMEY

GROUP 91 ARCHITECTS' FRAMEWORK PLAN FOR TEMPLE Bar contains the following statement of intent: 'This framework plan comprises a policy and a series of outline or illustrative architectural proposals designed to stimulate the renewal of Temple Bar and secure its future as the living heart of Dublin, and to serve as a model for inner city renewal. There is no one single solution; rather a flexible series of integrated responses is suggested, to release the dynamic potential of Temple Bar, while reinforcing its unique sense of place in our capital city.'

The plan avoided any large-scale building proposals and instead was based on the consolidation of the existing character and the conservation of the urban fabric. Two key ingredients for the integration of renewal proposals were the emphasis given to the creation of urban spaces as a contribution to the public realm of the city, and the importance of residential development in the regeneration of the living city.

In the extensive discussions and intensive analyses that followed from the adoption of the framework plan, certain elements emerged as 'immutables' and particular projects were recognised as essential, the achievement of which would have a propelling effect on the overall development plan.

Group 91 was commissioned by Temple Bar Properties to carry out a number of these flagship projects, and the realised schemes can now be compared with the aspirations of the initial competition proposals.

The development of the Dublin Corporation property portfolio to the west of Parliament Street has been treated as a second phase in Temple Bar Properties' building programme, and the framework plan has been re-cast to take into account the results of the archaeological investigations and the requirement for substantial residential development in scale with the mediaeval pattern of the site, which lay within the original city walls. The framework plan had been explicitly described in the competition report as 'not a rigid master-

Aerial view of Temple Bar showing the major urban interventions – (left to right) Meeting House Square, Curved Street and Temple Bar Square

PERMEABILITY

1. Fleet Street / Essex Street as primary link between Trinity and Christchurch • Existing pattern reinforced.

2. New pedestrian bridge taps potential movement from the northside into Meetinghouse Square and east west link Temple Bar becomes inner city focus.

3. Alleys, lanes, arcades, cut through existing blocks to permeate whole precinct • Variety of alternative routes created.

4. A new street made to facilitate indirect east / west links. A curved wall of shops in a new student quarter.

5. Parliament Street reinstated as north / south link to City Hall and Dublin Castle • Potential of City Hall as focus realised.

A COMMUNITY OF 3,0

A TOU

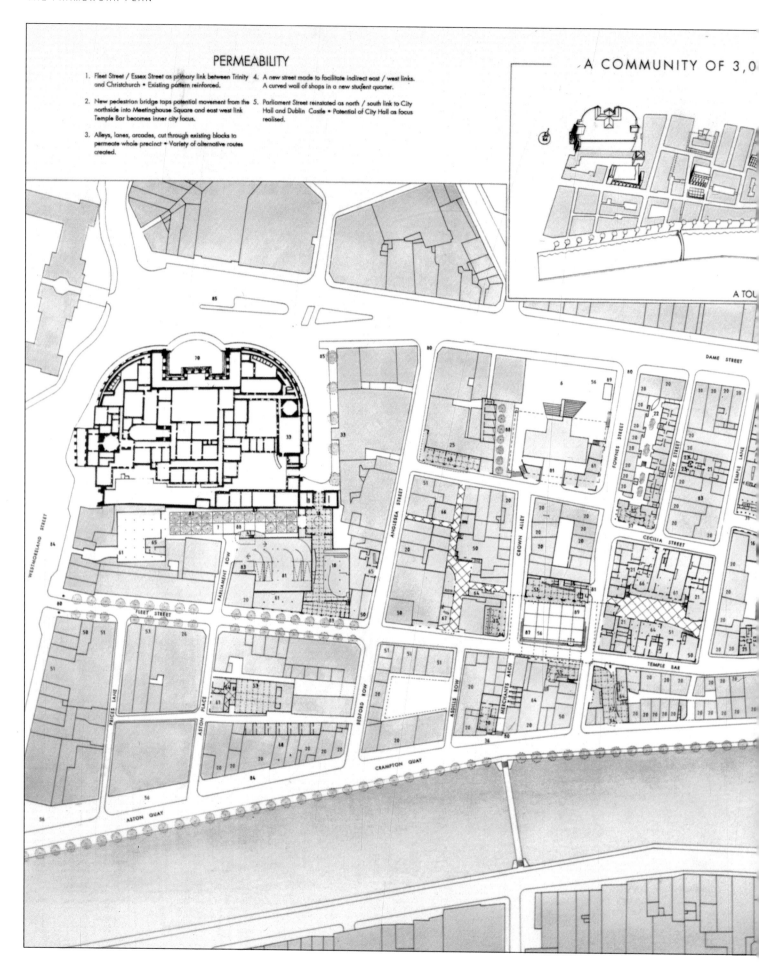

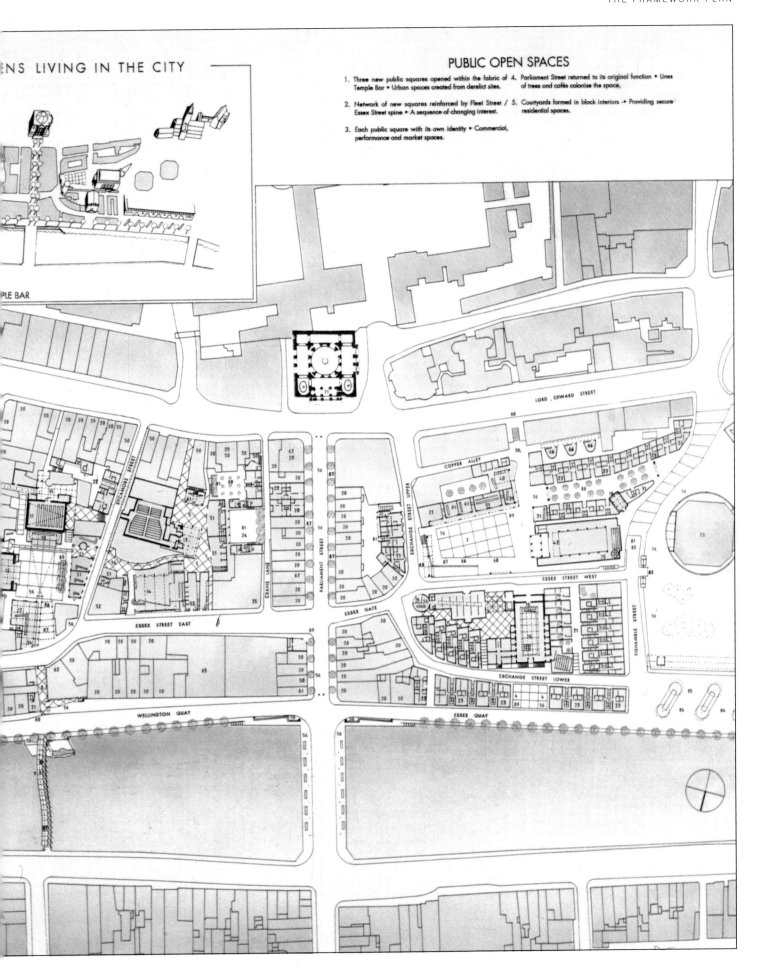

ENS LIVING IN THE CITY

PLE BAR

PUBLIC OPEN SPACES

1. Three new public squares opened within the fabric of
   Temple Bar • Urban spaces created from derelict sites.

2. Network of new squares reinforced by Fleet Street /
   Essex Street spine • A sequence of changing interest.

3. Each public square with its own identity • Commercial,
   performance and market spaces.

4. Parliament Street returned to its original function • Lines
   of trees and cafés colonise the space.

5. Courtyards formed in block interiors • Providing secure
   residential spaces.

LORD EDWARD STREET

COPPER ALLEY

SYCAMORE STREET

EXCHANGE STREET UPPER

CRANE LANE

PARLIAMENT STREET

ESSEX STREET WEST

FISHAMBLE STREET

ESSEX STREET EAST

ESSEX GATE

EXCHANGE STREET LOWER

WELLINGTON QUAY

ESSEX QUAY

plan to be realised in a literal fashion. Rather it is an integrated series of illustrative proposals – a design guide – bound together within a flexible framework which will evolve during the renewal of Temple Bar.' The revisions to the plan for the western end of Temple Bar are evidence of that flexibility at work, with the most significant change being the removal of the Market Square – the third public square in the series proposed under the framework plan. The public space proposed at the corner of Exchange Street Upper and Essex Street West has been replaced by a closer grid of residential streets with, Essex Street West leading to the public gardens associated with the new Civic Offices.

The principal urban components of Group 91's framework plan were the creation of new public spaces and buildings, the establishment of a strong east-west pedestrian route through the centre of the quarter, the integration of a mixture of cultural, commercial and residential uses, and the linking of Temple Bar into the rest of the city on a north-south axis.

NEW PUBLIC SPACES AND BUILDINGS

TEMPLE BAR SQUARE

The competition sketches show the south side of the square bounded by a four-storey terrace, creating a backdrop to the bustle of city life. The public square has been realised substantially unchanged from the original proposals. The building design has evolved, to reflect the incremental nature of the adjoining streets. The form of the building can be understood as less of a singular set-piece and more as part of the continuity of the scale of the surrounding street fabric.

The initial framework proposal involved the demolition and rehousing of the Bad Ass Café. However, the pizza restaurant was one of the pioneering businesses in the Temple Bar story and many people had become attached to the building which housed the enterprise. The saw-tooth, shed-roof structure is now a listed building, and the Temple Bar Square project both skirts the structure and extends the café space.

This lived-in space is intended to provide a side-step breathing space from the busy north-south route across the Ha'penny Bridge. It has a threshold effect which encourages westward pedestrian movement within Temple Bar, enhancing the east-west mid-block route. Commercial and residential mixed-use occupancy is clearly legible in the composition of the façade. Although at the time of writing the south side of the square remains a vacant site, the function, form and programme of the completed project are consistent with the aspirations of the initial idea.

MEETING HOUSE SQUARE AND PODDLE BRIDGE

The surface car park off Sycamore Street had been earmarked as a public space in the competition brief, arising out

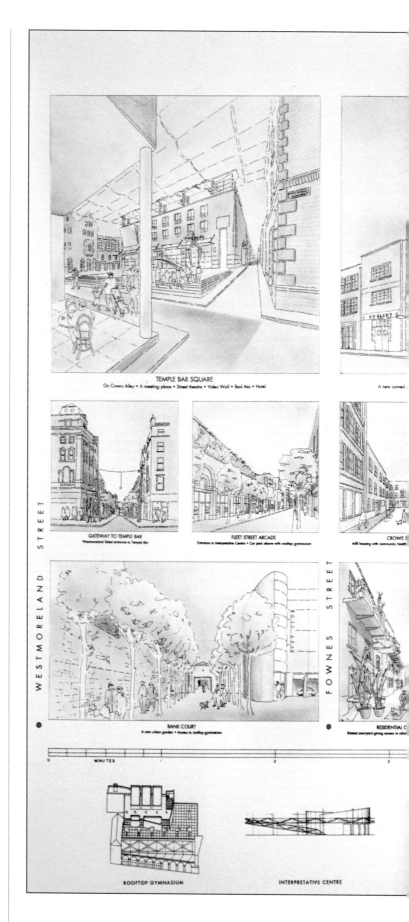

'A Walk through Temple Bar'
Temple Bar Framework Plan, 1991 (Group 91)

LK THROUGH TEMPLE BAR

R LANE
Street • Access to student housing in mid block

MEETING HOUSE SQUARE
Refurbished Meeting Houses • Indoor & outdoor performances • Cinema • Site of Dubh Linn • Tourist Office

MARKET SQUARE
Viking Museum & new housing define a market space • Country / flea market • On route to Christchurch

TEMPLE LANE ARCADE
Mixed use courtyard • Cafés & jewellery workshops • Residential above

ESSEX STREET
Project Arts Centre • Entrance to Olympia Theatre via Crampton Court

EAST ESSEX STREET
View across Parliament Street to Museum Tower

CATHEDRAL CLOSE
Tree lined residential street rising to Christchurch Cathedral • Tourist route

EUSTACE STREET

PODDLE BRIDGE
Pedestrian bridge joins Wellington Quay at the mouth of the Poddle.

NORTH - SOUTH LINK
Jervis Street to Fleet / Essex Streets and Meeting House Square

CRANE LANE
Studio apartments around raised garden • Car parking below

PARLIAMENT STREET

ST. MICHAEL'S & JOHN'S
The Viking Museum • New public space upon the Quays • Riverside apartments over commercial

FISHAMBLE STREET

TOURIST OFFICE PORTICO

PROJECT ARTS CENTRE

ARTISTS STUDIOS

LIFFEY SEAT

PODDLE BRIDGE

MUSEUM TOWER

of Dublin Corporation's Area Action Plan for Temple Bar. The former Quaker Meeting House was in the course of being refurbished for cinema and other uses, and was under construction at the time of the competition. The Action Plan had proposed a pedestrian route through the former Presbyterian Meeting House (subsequently developed as The Ark) to access a new public space flanked by the two meeting houses. Group 91's plan shifted the emphasis for the proposed east-west route by upgrading the significance of Fleet Street/ Temple Bar / Essex Street, and therefore it followed that Meeting House Square should support the primary route by means of a strong relationship with Essex Street. At a larger urban scale, the alignment of Jervis Street across the river generated the proposal for the Poddle Bridge to connect the new heart of Temple Bar with the wider dimensions of the city.

The Poddle Bridge was the subject of a lengthy planning process, and the covered curvilinear pedestrian bridge was refused planning permission at appeal. Without the bridge connection, one of the fundamental urban design principles of permeability and north-south linkage has been frustrated, and Meeting House Square has been deprived of its intended relationship with the River Liffey and the north side of the city.

As a result of practical constraints, the intended pedestrian way from Foster Place to Fleet Street also fell by the wayside, with the result that another opportunity for north-south permeability was not realised. Thus two of the proposed new north-south pedestrian routes have been abandoned or at best postponed. That Foster Place should remain simply as a beautiful backwater may be accepted without too many misgivings, but the bridge across the river to Meeting House Square was an indispensable element of the original urban design strategy.

Temple Bar Properties' Framework of Cultural Uses – a strategic document adopted by the company in 1992 – set out a programme of cultural uses which involved a mixture of refurbished or new buildings for existing or new Temple Bar cultural activities. The brief for Meeting House Square was developed to become a focus of cultural activity within Temple Bar.

In its cultural framework plan, Temple Bar Properties identified the need for specific cultural provision for children. The plan of the former Presbyterian Meeting House was reinstated in a new building with this brief, behind the restored street façade, and the large door at the rear of the stage allows for outdoor performance to an audience in the square. The Photography Centre brief re-locates the Gallery of Photography, already established on Wellington Quay, and combines the National Library Photography Archive in a shared building with the Dublin Institute of Technology School of Photography. The mixed use buildings forming the Sycamore Street frontage include the Gaiety School of Acting and a café opening onto the square. By means of

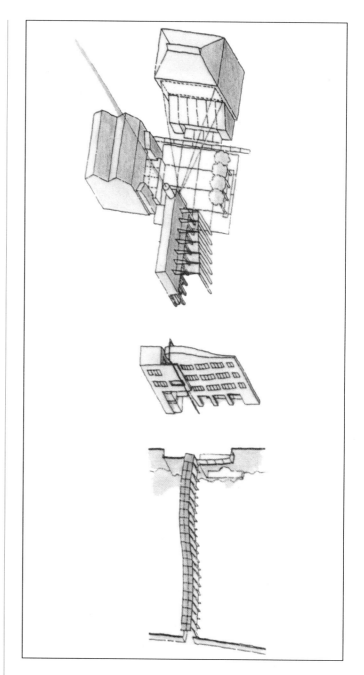

'North-South Link'
Temple Bar Framework Plan, 1991

these well-defined uses, the original idea of Meeting House Square as an urban room enlivened by theatrical performance and cinema projection has been realised. The public square has been designed to allow for a wide range of informal and seated performances, and the four routes of entry connect the square with the surrounding street pattern.

The Photography Archive / DIT building was designed to have a strong visual relationship with the cross axis of Parliament Street at the intersection with Essex Street. Group 91, therefore, proposed the demolition of Nos.33/34 Essex Street East in order to strengthen the connection of the new square with the street. Differences of opinion with the client

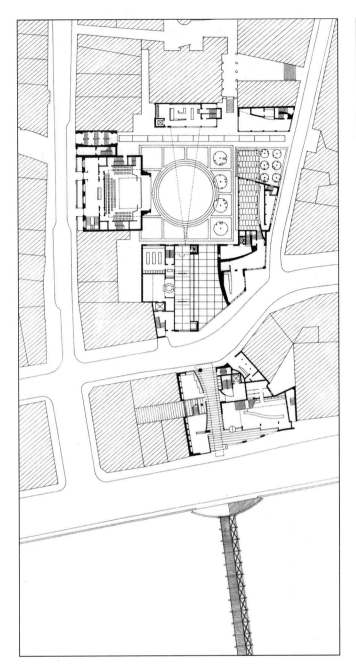

*Meeting House Square
and Poddle Bridge*

MIXED DEVELOPMENT

The Printworks, one of a series of mixed-use developments commissioned by Temple Bar Properties within the overall context of the framework plan, realises one of the key proposals for a new type of residential integration within the existing city block. The principle of the raised court allows ground-floor commercial activity to co-exist with first-floor social space for upper-floor apartments. The as-built scheme has a more complex configuration than the infill block shown on the framework plan. The initially simple model was adapted to take advantage of the available area and the central courtyard organises the awkward site geometries into a coherent shared space.

CURVED STREET

The proposal for a new street connecting Temple Lane and Eustace Street was a crucial component of the framework plan. The competition brief had emphasised the need for increased pedestrian permeability, and the Group 91 strategy was to invest in the existing street and lane network rather than restructure the area with internal courts and passages. The creation of Curved Street was representative of the commitment to the given urban order. The street was laid out to allow for the retention of surrounding listed buildings, and it swerves between its neighbours, setting up a meandering route in parallel with the direct east-west route of Temple Bar / Essex Street.

The competition drawings indicated that recording studios might be housed in Curved Street in continuation of the established uses in Temple Lane, and Temple Bar Music Centre has indeed emerged from the shell of the warehouses to provide a new venue, rehearsal spaces and recording facilities. The Arthouse multi-media centre occupies the southern side of the street, and the two complementary buildings create a light and open street with the common theme of providing facilities for performance and media-related arts. The original sketches for the street, prepared in the absence of any particular programme, anticipate the character of the as-built scheme, where modern architectural design can be seen in counterpoint to the 18th- and 19th-century buildings of Eustace Street and Temple Lane.

PEDESTRIAN WALKWAY

Across Eustace Street, the new pedestrian archway to Meeting House Square links the square directly to Curved Street, and from there a zig-zag via Cecilia Street connects back to Temple Bar Square. These three interventions form a new urban sequence which gives concrete expression to the strategies of the framework plan, and represents a constructed and coherent argument for the importance of public space in contemporary city life.

could not be resolved by consensus, and Temple Bar Properties required the listed two-storey brick building to be retained and refurbished. The dynamic curvilinear containment of the Photography Archive forecourt is one happy consequence of the retention of the existing building, but the obscured relationship with Parliament Street is its less than ideal corollary.

Parliament Street itself has been upgraded by widening the pavements, planting trees and calming the traffic. With the introduction of a variety of new street-level cafés, shops and upper-floor apartments, this grand street has been restored to its proper significance within the city centre.

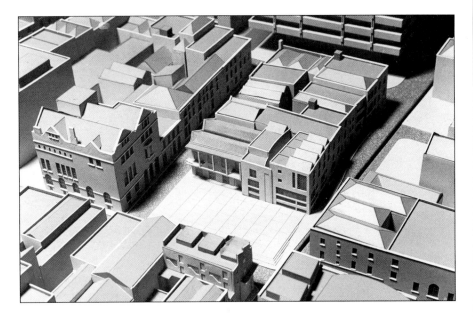

Temple Bar Square

GROUP 91 / GRAFTON ARCHITECTS

Temple Bar Square is the junction of one of the main north-south pedestrian routes, linking Temple Bar with the rest of the city. The square is really a widening of this route, a place to reorientate the pedestrian within Temple Bar itself.

The combination of public, retail and residential uses in Temple Bar Square reflects the framework plan's fundamental conviction about the need for integrated urban design, reflecting the complexity and diversity of city life. The development comprises a public space, five commercial units of varying sizes, and nine residential units.

The two main materials of the building are engineering brick trimmed with metal. The finish to the surface of the square and the residential courtyard is Donegal quartzite – a pale green-grey stone. This stone is brought into each apartment, where each kitchen worktop is honed Donegal quartzite.

The seats on the square are also of the this material. They are designed so as to appear as if they were pushed up out of the earth from the surface of the square itself. The steps, which take the slope of the site into account, are thick chunks of quartzite.

There are three large light masts to the west of the square. The three stainless steel bollards on the eastern edge mirror the proportions of the masts and the litter bins to the west.

Temple Bar Square is unique in our city. It is a new public space with no other agenda than to provide the citizens with an outdoor 'room', which acts as a backdrop to the lively urban culture which gives this district its character.

TEMPLE BAR SQUARE

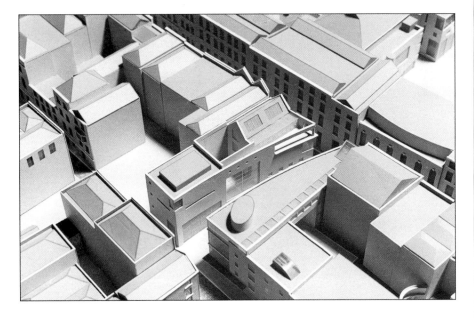

Curved Street

GROUP 91 / SHAY CLEARY ARCHITECTS

The street has a limestone surface and the pattern is orthogonal with the urban block, to emphasise the curve of the street. It falls from south to west, following the natural topography of the site, with an indented channel on the west side. The limestone setts are 300mm square, and the pattern forms continuous lines across the street to emphasise width. There are four steel bollards at either end of the street, two of which are demountable for service access. At the entrances to Arthouse and the Temple Bar Music Centre on either side, street and inside levels are the same to emphasise continuity.

The street lighting is suspended from rails at parapet level on each of the buildings. Lighting is designed to be indirect, with lights on each building lighting the building opposite. In addition, there are four uplighters embedded at street level outside Arthouse to emphasise the structure of the elevation.

The main entrance to Arthoouse is flanked by two video walls, enabling continuous performances onto the street. There are also events services (for example to provide for additional lighting, sound, etc) in recessed chambers in the street surface, which can be exploited for a variety of outdoor performance and exhibition purposes. Loudspeakers are recessed at the main entrance which also support this exhibition function.

At the ends of the street, both buildings have vertical rails which can be used to erect canvas 'ends', along with a canvas roof, to allow the street to act as an outdoor room for special events.

CURVED STREET

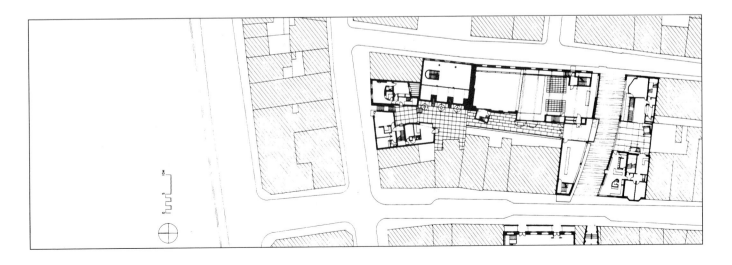

Pedestrian Archway

GROUP 91 / SHANE O'TOOLE AND MICHAEL KELLY ARCHITECTS

No.11 Eustace Street, next door to The Ark, is the location of the new pedestrian archway linking Curved Street with Meeting House Square. 11 Eustace Street is a two-bay, four-storey-over-basement house and dates from about 1730. The brick façade and stone doorcase are not original to the house, but were added during the 19th century. The house contains a rare, early timber-panelled stair hall and staircase which will be conserved in the refurbished building.

The pedestrian archway – the only 'internal' section of the meandering east-west route – is a tapering, stone-lined space, formed within the body of the original house.

The cascading steps are of Carlow granite, and the walls of the archway are of white limestone, into which is set cast glass, lit from behind.

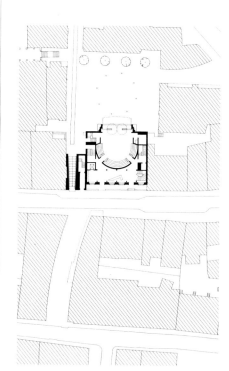

Meeting House Square

GROUP 91 / PAUL KEOGH ARCHITECTS

Meeting House Square is on the converging axes of several pedestrian routes through Temple Bar. It is part of a new urban sequence running from Curved Street, through the arched entrance on Eustace Street, into Meeting House Square, out on to Essex Street East.

Located on the site of a surface car-park, the square takes its name from buildings occupying two of its four sides – the Presbyterian Meeting House (1728) and the nineteenth-century former Quaker Meeting House, transformed in 1992 into the Irish Film Centre. The edges of the square are formed by a group of cultural facilities – The Ark on the east side, new buildings for photography uses on the north and south, and a new mixed-use building, accommodating café at ground-floor level, and the Gaiety School of Acting on upper floors.

Essentially an outdoor room, the square is intended to be used as an open-air performance space celebrating all forms of contemporary culture, including music and theatre performances staged from The Ark, and film screenings projected onto the screen façade of the Gallery of Photography from the Photographic Archive building.

The surface of the square is of Wicklow granite, with limestone at the entrance to the Photographic Archive, delineating a route from Essex Street East. The lighting on the square has been designed to complement the cultural brief, with stage lighting mounted at a high level on the perimeter, and a circle of uplighters set in the centre of the square. Trees and specially designed furniture have also been installed.

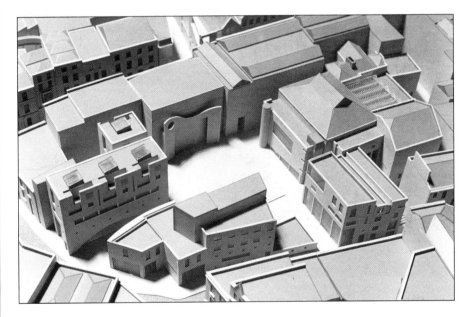

MEETING HOUSE SQUARE

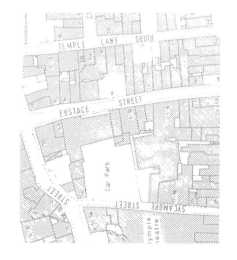

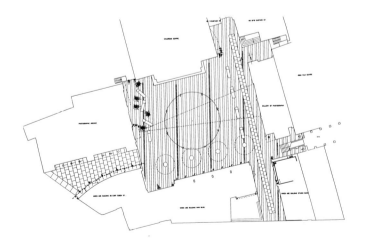

MEETING HOUSE SQUARE

Phase 2

WEST OF PARLIAMENT STREET

T HE NATURE OF THE MODIFICATIONS TO THE URBAN FRAMEWORK PLAN FOR THE WESTERN sector of Temple Bar has already been discussed by John Tuomey above (on pages 88-95). Following a process of brief development and discussion with the officials of the planning authority, a revised framework for Phase 2 (west of Parliament Street) was adopted by Temple Bar Properties in 1995, and a set of related schemes of mostly residential and retail developments will be lodged with the local authority for planning permission in Summer 1996.

As with the rest of Temple Bar, the framework plan for the area west of Parliament Street has a particular set of urban, architectural, social, cultural and environmental parameters, which are described in more detail below. Like all of Temple Bar Properties' commercial projects, the actual schemes of development undertaken will be subject to an overall discipline of returning a surplus of 5% to the Exchequer. The Phase 2 development on this site has also been subject to certain conditions of sale by the vendor (Dublin Corporation), requiring 30% of the development to be provided to the local authority for social housing purposes.

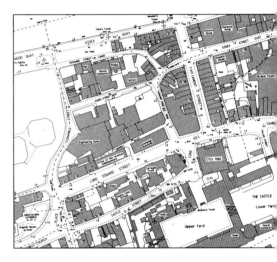

Ordnance Survey, 1991

ARCHITECTURAL BRIEF

The Development Brief for the western sector of Temple Bar is being realised by five architectural practices in accordance with the following objectives set out by Temple Bar Properties:

- To seek the achievement of architectural excellence in all its development projects
- To confront and resolve critical contemporary urban design issues in an exemplary manner
- To create a sense of community identity in a modern urban context
- To respect the archaeological and historical integrity of the area

Five architectural practices were selected from among the original entrants to the Temple Bar framework plan competition in order to achieve design diversity, but operating within a clear framework of uses.

SOCIAL BRIEF

The provision of a mixed residential/workshop/retail/market development on the main site bordered by Fishamble Street, Exchange Street and Copper Alley, grouped around raised private courtyards, and divided into two blocks around a planned north-south street, is the central brief for this part of the development. The two elements of the main site are divided by the line of the future north-south street, and the development is to be planned such that the street is capable of being

Phase 2 – west of Parliament Street – as seen in the original model

realised in the future. Workshop/retail and market accommodation will be at ground-floor level along the site perimeter.

The aim is to provide residential accommodation for approximately 500 people, on the upper floors, in a mixture of one-, two- and three-bedroom apartments. Thirty percent social housing is to be provided on lands west of Parliament Street.

CULTURAL BRIEF

The development will incorporate a comprehensive archaeological programme, respecting the historical importance and integrity of this area. The main elements of this programme are:

- the resolution of certain key sites (by means of a publicly-accessible dig, to be viewed from the new infill building in Dublin's Viking Adventure)
- the design of new buildings above the layer of archeological deposits
- the publication of the results of archeological excavation.

Public art will feature in this development, as in Phase 1, and an artist will be appointed to each of the design teams on their respective projects.

ENVIRONMENTAL BRIEF

Maximising the opportunities offered by the scale of the development, the frame-work brief articulates a policy to build in an environmentally responsible manner. This involves, for example, the collection, storage and distribution of solar energy, rain water and other 'free' environmental elements; the use where possible of natur-al ventilation systems; the minimisation of thermal and other energy loss; the utilisa-tion of materials whose production has entailed minimal environmental damage; and the design of effective building management and control systems (including waste management) for the optimal environmental effect.

The time-frame for the implementation of this second phase is two years from the date of receipt of planning approval.

LAURA MAGAHY
Manaing Director
Temple Bar Properties

Cultural Projects

INTRODUCTION

THE DEVELOPMENT PROGRAMME FOR TEMPLE BAR INCORPORATED A GROUP OF SPECIAL building projects dedicated to a range of artistic or cultural uses. These included the refurbishment of existing cultural buildings for the organisations already using them, the development of new buildings for existing Temple Bar cultural organisations, and the introduction of new cultural activities to the area – whether by relocating those already based elsewhere, or by direct initiative on the part of Temple Bar Properties or others.

Each of these projects is described in the section that follows, first by the architect responsible for designing it, then (in the case of buildings which have been in use for some months or years) by the director of the company which now operates it.

Two additional projects are described in addition to the nine already developed by Temple Bar Properties: the Irish Film Centre and Project Arts Centre. The IFC development was initiated by the Irish Film Institute and undertaken by Irish Film Centre Building Ltd under a preliminary phase. The development works were completed by Temple Bar Properties.

Project Arts Centre is the final element of the cultural development programme to be initiated, and will be undertaken by Temple Bar Properties as part of Phase 2. It was originally intended that the project would be developed as part of a single construction programme with the adjacent 19th-century Olympia Theatre, but the latter project was dropped from the programme when the operators of the building adopted an alternative development strategy for commercial reasons.

The cultural projects are featured in the order in which they were opened:

Irish Film Centre	September 1992
Designyard	December 1993
Temple Bar Gallery and Studios	November 1994
Black Church Print Studio	March 1995
The Ark	September 1995
Gallery of Photography	September 1995
Arthouse	November 1995
Temple Bar Music Centre	May 1996
Dublin's Viking Adventure	June 1996
National Library Archive /	
DIT School of Photography	July 1996
Project Arts Centre	(at planning)

Cultural Projects

IRISH FILM CENTRE

O'DONNELL AND TUOMEY ARCHITECTS

The Irish Film Centre is located in the former Quaker headquarters in Dublin. This consisted of a group of buildings varying in age, condition and architectural quality, gathered around a covered space which was once an open yard. It occupies the centre of a city block and has no significant street frontage, but it has narrow routes of access from Eustace Street, Dame Street and Sycamore Street.

The building accommodates all aspects of film culture. It includes two cinemas, the national film archive, a bookshop, restaurant, bar, classrooms and offices for various organisations.

The brief was, to some extent, determined by what was possible within the existing Quaker buildings. This brief was quite fluid, as during the five years between purchase of the site and commencement of construction, the organisations which would occupy the building changed and multiplied. It quickly became clear that, within the budget available, it would not be possible to restore and repair the buildings fully and provide all the accommodation required by the client. It was agreed that the technical quality of projection, sound, seating, etc, would be to the highest standard, as would the public foyer and entrance areas, so any compromises would have to be made in other areas.

The result was that decorative work only was carried out in some parts of the old buildings, in the knowledge that repair and the addition of services to these would be needed in the future. Other areas of the old building were repaired or restored with great care, in particular in areas where it would be difficult to do work in the future without disruption, or where the extent of disrepair posed a risk.

Parts of the existing building were clearly suited to the proposed use, both in their general character and spatial qualitiy. Both of the cinemas are housed within the walls of existing rooms, as are the bar and some offices. New elements have been installed within these rooms to accommodate the new functions. The principal areas of new building are the foyer, the projection room and the archive.

A new steel sign-box with neon illumination projects over the old door to the Quaker headquarters on Eustace Street,

Entrance on Eustace Street

opposite – The roof-lit foyer at the centre of the IFC complex

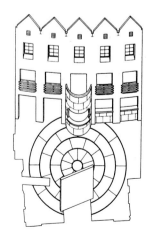

111

Irish Film Archive

*Axonometric of the complex from Sycamore Street
(with the Archive at the bottom left)*

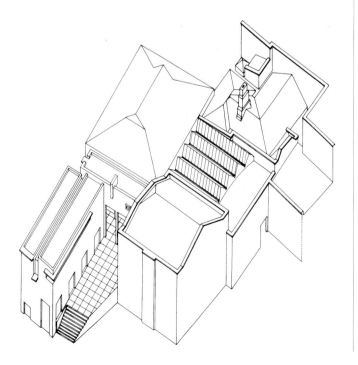

indicating the entrance to the Film Centre. A long, tunnel-like corridor leads from the main entrance in Eustace Street, under another building, into the foyer. Its length is illuminated by a ladder-like floor light in mild steel with 25mm etched glass over neon lights. Its walls make a gallery for film posters and reviews.

The foyer occupies the central space, with a new glass roof installed at high level. Three sides of the courtyard are formed by existing buildings. On the fourth side is a new three-storey building, housing offices, restaurant and information / box-office.

The materials in the new building and the roof and floor of the foyer accentuate the sense of an external public place. The floor is limestone, in concentric circles separated by mild steel bands. The new plaster walls are coloured with natural ochre and cobalt pigments, and elements within the walls are made of oiled and waxed mild steel with walnut leaning rails and counter tops.

The larger cinema is housed in the former meeting room, the most significant part of the old building. This dated from the early 19th century, and showed evidence of having been changed frequently throughout that century, with the walls raised, windows blocked up and new ones added. The Film Centre was seen as adding another layer to the life of this building. The room was stark and severe in its architecture, with some more florid details added in the late 19th century.

A maple cabinet was added, which lets sound pass between the slats to the dense layers of acoustic insulation behind. All the technical requirements are housed in this piece of furniture, building nothing into the architecture of the room. The windows behind remain in place, blocked up on the outside to exclude sound and light. It is possible that the screen cabinet might be removed and the windows reopened in the event of a further change of use.

A new building on Sycamore Street houses the archival functions. It is made in smooth red brick with steel windows and concrete elements. This small infill building is the only part of the Film Centre which has a presence on the public street. It has a narrow front to Sycamore Street, and its long side extends into the site, forming one side of a new raised courtyard. A drop in level across the site allows the film storage to be at street level, one floor below the public access, which is level with the other public facilities. The limestone-clad projection box is at high level between the external walls of the two cinemas and the archive block. The slender columns which support it make an informal portico, with a blue neon line on the stone soffit, connecting the entrance to a wide flight of steps down to the new public space of Meeting House Square.

O'DONNELL AND TUOMEY
Architects

The 250-seater Cinema 1 housed in the former Quaker Meeting Room

Ticket kiosk made of mild steel

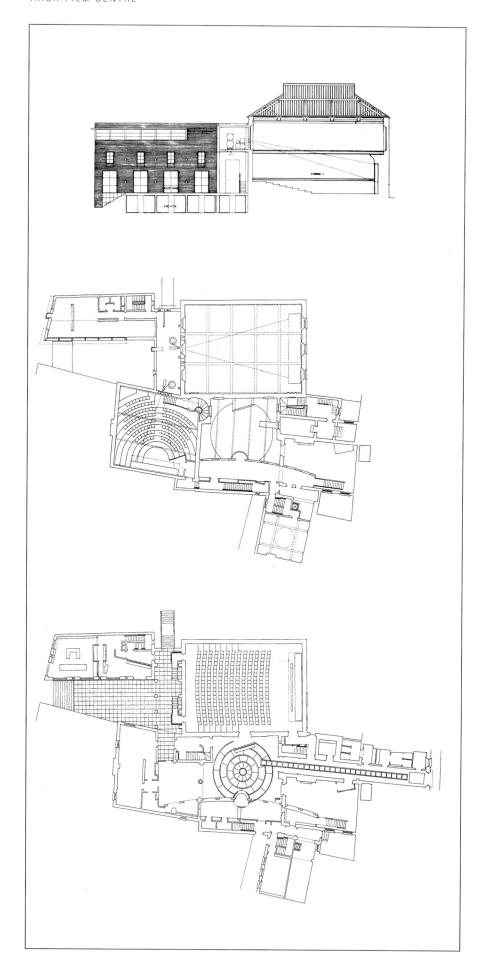

Section
First floor plan
Ground floor plan

opposite

View of the foyer in daylight and in the
glow of the neon lighting

Custom-designed wall display and
steel seat in foyer

above – IFC restaurant overlooking the foyer
below – IFC bar (before alterations)

opposite – The 'projection box' on the Sycamore Street side

The Irish Film Centre opened in September 1992. It is impossible to estimate how many people have visited the building since then, but it has truly become what it was intended to be – a cultural meeting place and crossroads. This will be even more the case when Meeting House Square becomes fully functional and the flows of traffic through the Centre are increased and diversified.

One of the most striking areas in the Film Centre complex is the long entrance with its floor lighting looking like a strip of film, inviting further exploration. The central atrium, which is our foyer area, has a cosmopolitan, open-air atmosphere with its high glass roof, old and new walls, straight lines and curves, and modern steel furniture. The space transforms beautifully at night with the addition of tables, chairs, candle-light, gelled overhead lighting, and music.

The cinemas are nicely contrasting. The larger cinema, seating 260, is modern and comfortable, although the room retains many of the old details; the smaller cinema, seating 115, is steeply raked and retains its old roof timbers. Last year we adapted the bar area so that it is more conventional, with the old schoolroom atmosphere underscored by an open fire, wooden benches, tables and chairs.

The building as a whole works for the users in that they are led unobtrusively from one area to another, from an older ambience into a more modern one, from functional areas into spaces made for relaxation and social intercourse.

To date, the connection between the main building and our new archive building has been difficult to establish – only those who have had reason to visit the archive or the library have become fully aware of the extent of the Centre. The archive suffers from certain limitations in terms of space and development possibilities. It is not yet at full capacity, but we will need to look at ways in which new technology can facilitate conservation, storage and access in the future. The library is smaller than we would like. On the other hand, we do emphasise its specialist nature and the fact that it is now connected, through the Internet, with specialist libraries in other countries.

Unlike many of the cultural projects which have been developed in recent months in Temple Bar, the Irish Film Centre is now staffed by people who had little or no engagement with its development or, indeed, with the architects. Perhaps some of the architects' original concepts have been subverted. I think, however, that the strongest feeling we all share about the Irish Film Centre is pride: pride in its appearance, its versatility, and the fact that it has become an important space for everybody whose life is touched by the magic of film and the moving image.

SHEILA PRATSCHKE
Director
May, 1996

DESIGNYARD

FELIM DUNNE & ASSOCIATES /
ROBINSON KEEFE DEVANE ARCHITECTS

This 18th-century building – most recently home to the Head Gallery – was originally used as a china warehouse on its lower three floors, possibly with offices and caretakers rooms on the top floor. A triangular yard to the rear allowed daylight to all levels. This yard may once have been covered-in at first-floor level. The new uses of the refurbished building as an applied arts centre, with gallery space on the lower three floors, and meeting rooms and offices on the top floor, are clearly compatible with the original uses of the building.

When acquired by Temple Bar Properties in 1992, the building was in a semi-derelict condition. The brief required it be sensitively restored, reusing existing materials wherever possible. The brickwork to the front façade has been restored with the use of 'tuck' pointing. The use of tuck pointing arose during the 18th century in an effort to disguise any irregularities in the bricks. It is achieved by first pointing in a coloured mortar to match the brickwork, and then forming a small horizontal and vertical groove within the pointing to take 6mm of white lime putty, resulting in characteristic thin line pointing. The cast-iron columns and timber beams have been reinstated on each of the lower three floors, as originally. New windows, window linings and cills have been carefully reproduced, retaining the profile and mouldings of the original.

Four new monumental openings are set in the front wall at ground-floor level, completing the four-bay rhythm of the façade. A new shopfront is placed behind the façade, creating a street-side colonnade, secured at night with four large-scale wrought iron gates representing the cities of Dublin, Manhattan, Vienna and Madrid. These gates were forged in Dublin by Harry Page to a design by Kathy Prendergast, as part of the Temple Bar Public Art Programme. The gates represent a side-bar to Prendergast's work in progress, an expanding series (now 49) of pencil drawings of capital cities around the world, stripped of street names and text in the anatomical manner, for which she won the prestigious Premio Duernilia at the 1995 Venice Biennale.

The Jewellery Gallery at ground-floor level is a simple open hall, vaguely exterior in character, reflecting its public intention. Six luminescent containers, conceived to be objects in themselves, allow for unhindered viewing of the

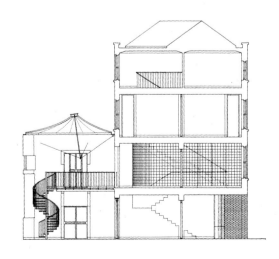

works displayed within them. These radiant containers organise the interior space they share, establishing a sense of place.

A serpentine mosaic inlay, commissioned from Sarah Daly to represent the Poddle river below, leads through the gallery to the triangular yard, now covered by a tented canopy. A metal stair and bridge rises from the tented yard to the first-floor Interiors Gallery. A new main stair continues in straight flights to the seminar room and offices above.

FELIM DUNNE
Architect

Although elegant and restrained in the streetscape, the building's conservation-conscious façade with its monumental gates does not immediately welcome the passing crowd. Despite its design as a public space, Designyard has required a considerable amount of public relations activity to familiarise our audience with it. However, once the public has established the building as a public domain, their delight on entering the ground-floor space is evident. Ironically, security has been more manageable for us than for neighbouring businesses as the building does not look readily accessible.

The understated nature of the two gallery spaces allows the work of a diverse range of designers/makers of jewellery, metalwork, ceramics, lighting, textiles and wood to be seen to its full advantage. The brief to the design team in this regard has been amply fulfilled.

The mosaic river, which begins at the *entrance to the building and runs through the ground-floor space, leads one to the spiral staircase in the yard area. This staircase gives access to the Interiors Gallery. It can, however, sometimes prove confusing to the public in the delineation between public and staff areas. It is a pity, due to the Poddle river flowing underneath the building, that it was not possible to install a lift. The first-floor gallery and seminar room are, therefore, not viable for disabled access.*

The seminar room/exhibition showroom, which is flooded with natural light, can quickly and easily move from being an exhibition area, to a meeting room, to a studio, etc. A space of this nature within a building is valuable for its flexibility. The building is currently being fully utilised. Future growth will require careful management.

DANAE KINDNESS
Director
May, 1996

opposite
top – Interiors Gallery (first floor)
bottom – Jewellery Gallery (ground floor)

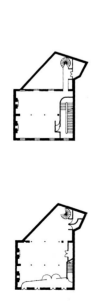
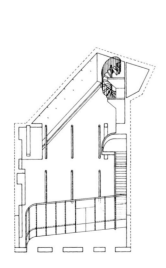
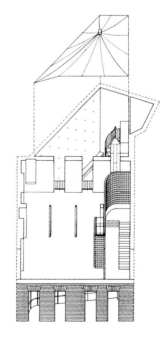

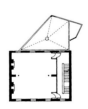

TEMPLE BAR GALLERY AND STUDIOS

McCULLOUGH MULVIN ARCHITECTS

In the early 1980s, Temple Bar Gallery and Studios, an organisation of artists, rented a disused shirt factory from CIÉ. Their shoestring activities – artists' studios, exhibition space, café, print workshop, sculptors' annex, etc – quickly began to contribute to the 'left bank' atmosphere for which Temple Bar has become famous. The early 20th-century industrial building, which extends through a block from Temple Bar on to the Liffey quays, provided a wonderful framework of spaces for artists to work in. However, the roof leaked, there was no heating in winter, in summer the glazed roof area was like a furnace, the original electrics did intermittent service, and a warren of passageways and studio partitions made it a potential firetrap.

The building has now undergone extensive refurbishment, and a new extension was constructed on an adjacent gap site to rebuild the corner. Thirty artists' studios in a range of sizes have been provided, the gallery space has been reorganised, and the artists have their own independent entrance off Fownes Street. There are showers and a small kitchen area for occupants' use, offices for gallery and studio administration on the top floor, and a new storage area in the basement.

Working with the mechanical and electrical engineers and the architects on the project, artist Darrell Viner created a link between the utilities (lift switch, running water) in the building and a series of blue lights installed in the roof of the building and in the pavement outside, which come on and off as the services in the building are used.

The gallery has been enlarged to twice the previous size and fronts on to Temple Bar and Temple Bar Square. A new 'shop window' draws the public in to view the exhibitions. Inside, new lighting systems have been installed, and the walls and ceilings strengthened to take the weight of heavy works or hanging pieces. Surfaces are simple and neutral. Beside the gallery, two sculptors' studios have large industrial doors on to the street, and are equipped with lifting beams for heavier fabrication.

A generous top-lit atrium space has been created to link the old and new parts of the building. This contains the artists' entrance at one end and the stairs at the other. A large oval

View down Fownes Street from Wellington Quay

Wellington Quay elevation

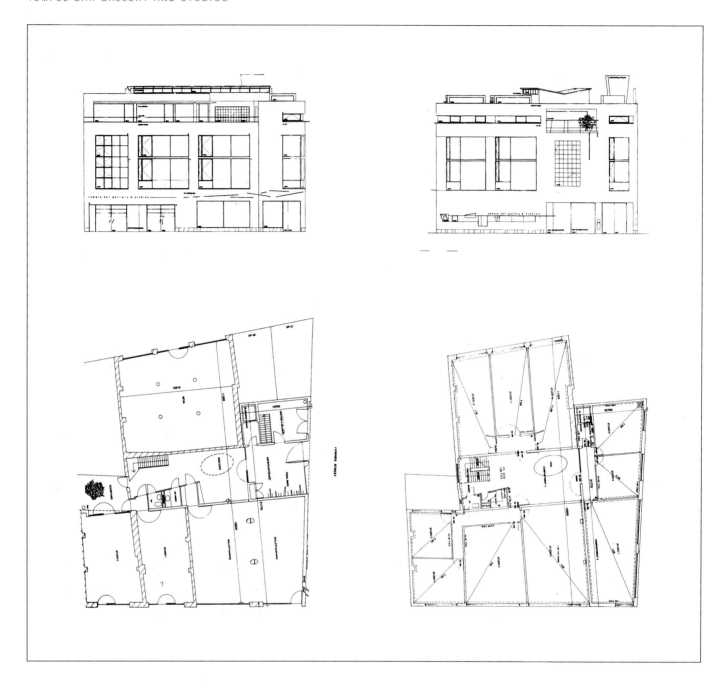

hole has been made through the ceiling of each storey, which allows light down from the new butterfly rooflight, and awkward canvases to be brought up and down by means of a hoist at the top.

Each studio has been given the maximum possible amount of light, and the top-floor studios – set back to reduce the bulk of the building on the street – open on to communal roof terraces to Temple Bar and the river.

The rooftop itself has been rebuilt to remove rotten timbers and rusting structural steelwork. The building now has heating and decent lighting, safe fire escapes and a lift for people with disabilities. The strategy has been to retain the 'factory' character of the spaces, with exposed floorboards

and minimum internal decorative features, while giving the studios a basic level of comfort and safety for artists to work in. The existing façades to Wellington Quay and Temple Bar are retained, with remedial work and new windows. The corner site becomes a 'bookend' to the block.

McCULLOUGH MULVIN
Architects

————

opposite
Artists' studios in the extensively refurbished building

Now that the shakedown period is over, it is obvious that Temple Bar Gallery and Studios has retained much of its original atmosphere within a vastly improved building, with more studios and an enlarged exhibition space. The physical building has crept into the language of the organisation in subtle ways. The oval void of the atrium inspired the new logo, and the quarterly newsletter is called Oval Office!

For the artists who use the studios, the effect of the development has been to transform their working environment. The individual studio spaces are more comfortable, better lit, and secure, and, just as important, they are supplemented by shared circulation spaces where the artists can meet, have a cup of coffee, or just take a break from the space where they are working intensively. The terraces on the top floor and the roof garden provide a recreational space, and many of the artists have commented on the extent to which they value this.

The atrium space through the core of the building is proving to have wider roles and uses, which may not have been fully evident at the design stage. It offers extensive hanging space for exhibitions, and even for more experimental uses, including performances and special events. It has already been used as an exhibition space by outside bodies, such as art colleges for their degree shows, and can be used in this way to generate much-needed revenue for the gallery and studios. The fact that this potential may not have been fully realised at design development stage, and that the atrium was, in fact, seen more as a private space for the artists, may result in some modification of the public access route from the gallery on the ground floor.

The fact that the gallery is on the street, like the Original Print Gallery next door, means that it is much more visible to the public and invites unplanned visits by passers-by. The building as a whole now has a far greater presence on the street, as part of the urban landscape. This is true at street level, but also on the upper floors, especially on the quays, where the dramatic terraced studios present a very striking image from the other side of the river.

Speaking as a newly appointed director who has just taken up responsibility for running Temple Bar Gallery and Studios, I feel that the 'karma' of this building is right for all kinds of exciting developments.

NORAH NORTON
Director
June 1996

———

The atrium and the oval

opposite – Brian Kennedy's 'Lagganstown Prints' hanging in the gallery

BLACK CHURCH PRINT STUDIO

McCULLOUGH MULVIN ARCHITECTS

Black Church Print Studio had operated elsewhere in the city until closed by a disastrous fire a number of years ago. A new building has been constructed for the Print Studio in Temple Bar, on the site of the former single-storey sculptors' annex to Temple Bar Gallery and Studios.

In urban terms, the building aimed to repair a piece of street by filling in a vacant lot in the dense network of buildings and streets in the area. Its neighbours are diverse – 18th-, 19th- and 20th-century buildings, all of different character. This building is contemporary, yet respectful of parapet heights, scale and plot sizes, so it becomes a modern yet sensitive contributor to the urban fabric of Temple Bar.

The footprint of the building is small enough not to require a lift. A single, curved staircase, extruded to the rear of the building, rises as a tower, visible from the river. The building provides three floors of print-making facilities – screen-printing, etching and lithography – with a print gallery at street level.

The Temple Bar façade of the building, gridded like a compositor's frame of typefaces, has a blank panel of white limestone to one side, with indented markings reminiscent of the stones used in the lithography process. There is a glass door to the gallery and a solid door to the print workshop areas. The solid door was part of the Temple Bar Public Art Programme, and was a collaboration between sculptor and printmaker Andrew Folan and architect Valerie Mulvin.

The façade above gallery level is pulled forward to allow a slit of light into the building and to provide users of the building with dramatic views up and down Temple Bar. The larger area of windows give maximum light to each printing floor. The top storey is set back to provide a roof terrace and to respect the scale of the street. To the rear, the large-scale industrial windows are composed in such a way as to provide maximum light to the laboratory-like facilities inside, and also to provide stunning views of the river and quays.

McCULLOUGH MULVIN
Architects

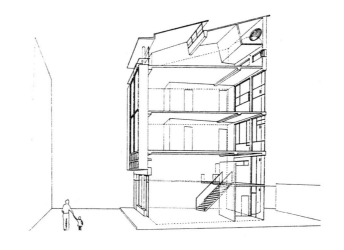

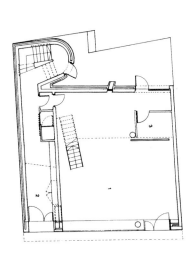
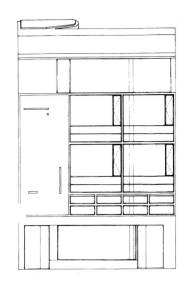
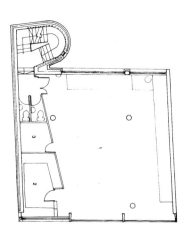

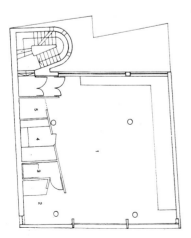

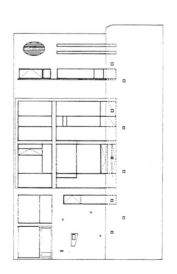

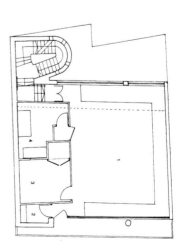

The Black Church Print Studio was designed with frequent consultation of the studio's representative at all stages of its conception and development. The result is a unique facility of major significance for Irish printmakers.

The Black Church Print Studio provides facilities for all of the disciplines of fine art printmaking, and also aims to promote the contemporary role of printmaking. Our location in Temple Bar is an excellent environment in which to develop our policy of integrating as much as possible with all of the visual arts, especially painting, sculpture, computer and installation art.

Our new premises accommodates not only the Original Print Gallery, but also printmaking facilities on three floors: etching, silk screen, lithography and relief, as well as a library and information service. Within the confines of a small site, the separation of the three main disciplines on different floors has created an excellent working environment.

The fact that essential services for each medium are adjacent to each studio space means that each floor can operate independently of the others, thereby minimising disruption to other working artists. The large windows at the front and back give maximum light, and extractor fans and other environmental features in the studio produce a unique facility where artists can work in calm, clean, bright and well-equipped surroundings.

The studio and gallery operate independently of one another, but can be interconnected to facilitate joint marketing or educational programmes.

NIAMH O'DONNELL
Administrator, Black Church Print Studio
June 1996

The gallery has been in use since October 1994, and the full potential of the space is still being explored. The double-height space, with mezzanine level, gives an interesting volume, which is ideal for large or challenging formats. The gallery is perceived as an important showcase for viewing contemporary print in Dublin. It has an enviable shopfront position from which to exhibit the 150 artists in its portfolio – most of them Irish.

SHEILA MILLS
Director, Original Print Gallery
May 1996

THE ARK

GROUP 91 / SHANE O'TOOLE AND MICHAEL KELLY ARCHITECTS

The brief for a children's centre in No.11a Eustace Street had, from the beginning, a dual function: the provision of a theatre, exhibition, workshop and ancillary spaces for the operation of The Ark, and the capacity for the theatre in the building to play on to Meeting House Square.

11a Eustace Street is the location of the former Presbyterian Meeting House (built in 1725), latterly a printing works and warehouse. Although included on List 1 of the planning authority's Development Plan, its entire interior (including roof, floors, stairs, walls, furniture) was gutted many decades ago. New floors and unsympathetic structural elements had been introduced, and the back wall extensively disfigured. All that remained of the original building was the six-bay façade to Eustace Street and the plan outline of the original building. This was the case forty years ago when Maurice Craig commented that it was the only surviving Presbyterian church of early date in Dublin: 'The façade survives, with rich segment-headed doors and windows framed in bolection mouldings of strongly English character (ca. 1685).'[1]

Despite extensive research into the history of the building, it proved impossible to identify the designer of this elaborate and handsome façade. The one version of the plan of the original Meeting House which could be found was the 1843 Ordnance Survey map. The original plan shows a long hall giving on to a galleried meeting room behind, and this became the model for the new design, which also incorporated the conservation, in very considerable detail, of the Eustace Street façade, under the direction of David Slattery. Conservation work included stripping away the 19th-century external render, wigging and tuck-pointing the Eustace Street brickwork and rebuilding the parapet. More than twenty layers of paint were removed from the Portland stone window surrounds. All ten window cills were replaced (several being recycled for other stone repairs to the façade) and the windows reinstated, complete with mitre-block details and crown glass.

The six-bay rhythm of the Eustace Street façade, with its load-bearing brickwork piers, is continued in the design of the new reinforced concrete structure of The Ark. The footprint of the original building is reinstated, as is, figuratively, the attic space, now a north-lit studio workshop

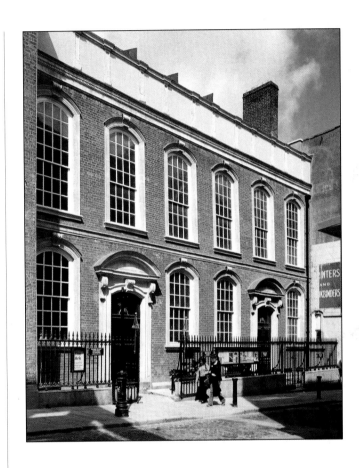

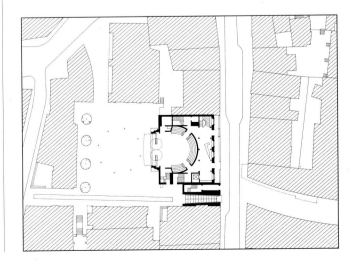

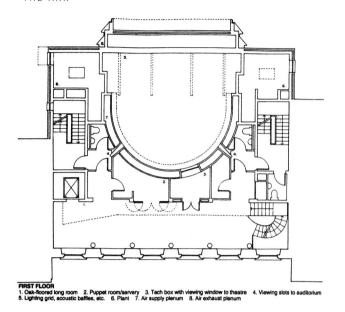

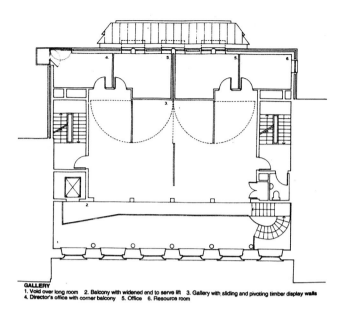

FIRST FLOOR
1. Oak-floored long room   2. Puppet room/servery   3. Tech box with viewing window to theatre   4. Viewing slots to auditorium
5. Lighting grid, acoustic baffles, etc.   6. Plant   7. Air supply plenum   8. Air exhaust plenum

GALLERY
1. Void over long room   2. Balcony with widened end to serve lift   3. Gallery with sliding and pivoting timber display walls
4. Director's office with corner balcony   5. Office   6. Resource room

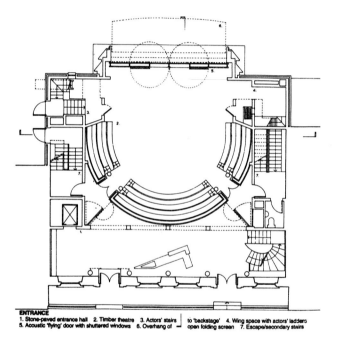

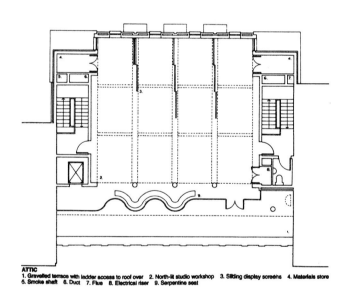

ENTRANCE
1. Stone-paved entrance hall   2. Timber theatre   3. Actors' stairs | to 'backstage'   4. Wing space with actors' ladders
5. Acoustic 'flying' door with shuttered windows   6. Overhang of ⌐   open folding screen   7. Escape/secondary stairs

ATTIC
1. Gravelled terrace with ladder access to roof over   2. North-lit studio workshop   3. Sliding display screens   4. Materials store
5. Smoke shaft   6. Duct   7. Flue   8. Electrical riser   9. Serpentine seat

concealed behind the front parapet. The Ark's new façade to Meeting House Square is more expressive. Faced in brick and stone, its non-structural nature is revealed by suspending it, so it hovers just above the paving of the square. The attic workshop may be read as The Ark's 'crown', while the great 'theatre curtain' doors which facilitate outdoor performances to the square are housed within the attached metal 'bellows', through which stale air from the theatre is exhausted.

Internally, the dominant materials and finishes are the original brickwork, in-situ concrete, oak, limestone, terracotta and galvanised steel. The choice of natural, self-coloured and durable materials was governed by a desire to imbue this modern children's building with civic or public qualities, as against the ubiquitous, plastic-filled, 'childish' environment of primary colours. By restricting the use of applied colour to the theatre alone, its effect there is heightened, evoking associations with an older tradition of popular auditoria.

SHANE O'TOOLE AND MICHAEL KELLY
Architects

[1] Maurice Craig, *Dublin 1660-1860*
(Dublin, 1952)

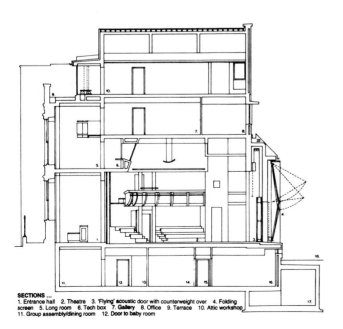

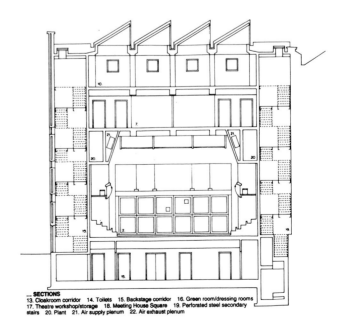

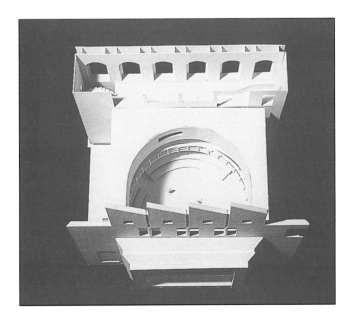

To date, there have been many thousands of end-users of The Ark. I refer in particular to the thousands of children for whom the centre was created and who have been using the spaces in the building and its various programmes. Children are demanding as a group of end-users, because their responses to a building will vary greatly according to their age and physical development. To date, they seem very comfortable and generally at ease with the building. If the front façade is imposing, the fact that there are three distinct major spaces (theatre, gallery and workshop) and three distinct minor spaces (reception area, basement eating area and long room) helps enormously to focus them and make the building manageable for them.

But, of course, children are not the only end-users of The Ark. There are also their teachers and parents, with different perspectives upon what makes the building work for them. There is the staff who work here on an on-going basis and in a range of capacities. There are the artists of all disciplines who make work here, creating and presenting performances, leading workshops. As actors, designers, technicians, musicians, sculptors, they are all interested in what the building can do for them. They may ignore the big picture, and seek to find out whether door width inhibits the size of a piece of sculpture to be created, or the placement of a lighting bar inhibits certain angles. There are the caterers with highly particular needs, and the cleaners whose perspective on the success of the building will be dominated by the surfaces and finishes on the materials called up by the architects. Insofar as it is reasonable for anyone to represent such a variety of end-user perspectives, I think that it is fair to say at this point that The Ark has proven to be eminently seaworthy.

At the time of writing, one significant use of The Ark has not yet been fully tested – the facility to open up the back doors of the theatre which face on to Meeting House Square and to give performances from the stage of The Ark to a public gathered in the square. This is a key public function, described by the architects as what the building 'gives back' to the city. The initial testing of this function is promising, but it will be July 1996 before we can be sure if that promise is fulfilled.

The Ark is an unusual project, not least because there was no prototype elsewhere which could be consulted during the design phase. Indeed it has itself quickly become such a case study for various European cities which have sent representatives to examine The Ark and its facilities.

What The Ark aspires to in its design and in its programming is quite simply to be a really good arts centre. What marks it out from most adult arts centres is attention to some of the physical realities of being a child – moderated, it must be said, by the exigencies of building regulations and, perhaps above all, the dedication of one whole floor of the building to a space where children can be the makers and doers, as well as lookers and listeners.

This floor, the workshop of The Ark, represents one of the great achievements of the building – the attainment of a kind of flexibility that is full-blooded rather than an anaemic 'can't make up our minds, can you give us a bit of everything' outcome, which characterises many arts spaces. To date, the workshop has embraced successfully a variety of different uses – display and interaction across a range of media, and has even served as an excellent rooftop restaurant for a dinner for The Ark's founding patrons. The workshop is certainly the surprise of the building, because when in the gallery, you believe you are at the top of the house. When you do penetrate all the way up, the wash of daylight which greets you when you reach the attic workshop lifts the spirits and helps the sense of being apart, which is conducive to concentrated work.

The theatre of The Ark is a jewel. It is an absolute realisation of the aspiration that informed the brief – to create an intimate room where children could be 'witnesses to' and not merely 'spectators at' performances. It is well-equipped technically, but it understands its responsibility to the audience and not only to the performer or technician. It was agreed from day one that it would not be a black box theatre, and it is neither a box not is it black. The configuration of the seating was debated long and hard. In the end, it was decided to make the seating part of the fixed furniture of the theatre space, and so the semi-circular wooden rows flow naturally from the semi-circular walls of the wrap-around cockpit that is the theatre of The Ark.

In summary, the design of The Ark grew from a lengthy and rich dialogue between myself, as representative of the client, Temple Bar Properties, and the architects, informed by a great deal of thinking and practice in the area of arts provision for young people. Now, as client-turned-end-user, I find that the building allows the freedom to plan the range and variety of cultural programmes which I believe should be embraced by an arts centre for children.

Martin Drury
Director
May 1996

––––

page 138 – The attic studio workshop, the first-floor area with gallery above, and the basement eating area

page 139 – The theatre – in use, in model form and with door opened to Meeting House Square

opposite – The entrance foyer of The Ark, recalling the long hall of the former Presbyterian Meeting House

GALLERY OF PHOTOGRAPHY

GROUP 91 / O'DONNELL AND TUOMEY ARCHITECTS

The Gallery of Photography is built against the blank brick wall of the Irish Film Centre, with its screen window facing north across Meeting House Square. The Portland stone façade is a light reflective element on the north-facing elevation, and is intended to harmonise with the brick buildings of the square. Many of the existing public buildings in central Dublin are faced in Portland stone, most notably City Hall and the Newcomen Bank.

The abstract elevation masks a complex sequence of interior spaces. Window openings are infilled with clear plate glass, translucent etched glass or zinc metal sheeting. The different materials create a variety of visual effects between transparency and opaqueness, which have associations with the nature of photography.

The entrance is at the busy pedestrian corner near the Irish Film Centre and proposed café on Sycamore Street, allowing for uninterrupted performances in the central public space.

Basement darkrooms provide for teaching and professional photography requirements. The ground floor contains office, bookshop and reception areas. The glass-enclosed stair leads to upper-level gallery spaces and a public roof terrace overlooking the square.

The gallery areas are designed to provide flexible space for a varied programme of exhibitions. Hinged and sliding screens can be positioned to double the available wall hanging space for larger exhibitions. The building had to be designed to allow for the occasional exclusion of daylight, without presenting a closed face to Meeting House Square. The large-scale window is the central organising element of the elevation, symbolising the camera lens and operating as a screen for films and photographs projected from the National Photography Archive opposite.

O'DONNELL AND TUOMEY Architects

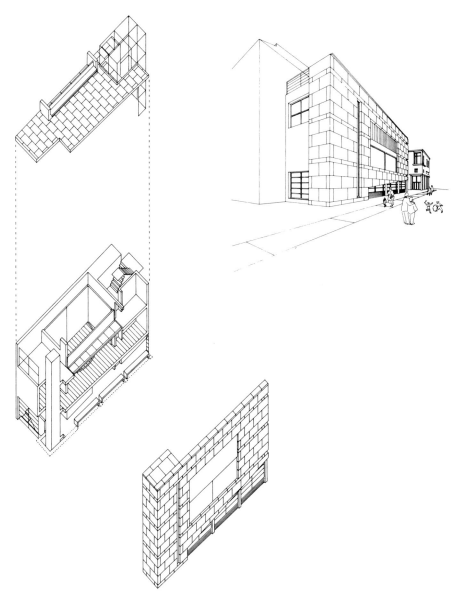

The Gallery of Photography was founded in 1978 and was formerly located at Wellington Quay, in the days when plans were afoot to turn the Temple Bar area into a bus depot. It was one of the original small independent arts organisations which helped to develop what has since become a vibrant area with an eclectic mix of activities.

In October 1995 we moved into a new purpose-built space in Meeting House Square. The gallery was involved in all stages of the design, which was a new and enormously challenging experience. With the benefit of hindsight, it would perhaps have been better to have waited until all building work was complete and the square open before moving in.

The gallery's exhibition areas have been designed to accommodate a wide range of sizes for both individual pieces and bodies of work. The main gallery is itself capable of changing shape dramatically and increasing its hanging capacity, both by means of shuttering the window and by movable walls (mimicking the internal movements in a basic box camera). The space has proved ideal in size for the majority of exhibitions that we have already shown. Storage space is a problem that will have to be resolved in the next few months.

One new feature of the gallery is the provision of darkrooms which can accommodate either groups or individuals, amateurs, students or professionals. There has always been a demand for good quality facilities, and we are now in a position to offer this service and to extend our existing and outreach programmes.

We are confident that this wonderful new gallery will, for the first time, give photography a suitable viewing environment and allow it to take its proper place in Ireland's cultural life.

Christine Redmond
Director
May 1996

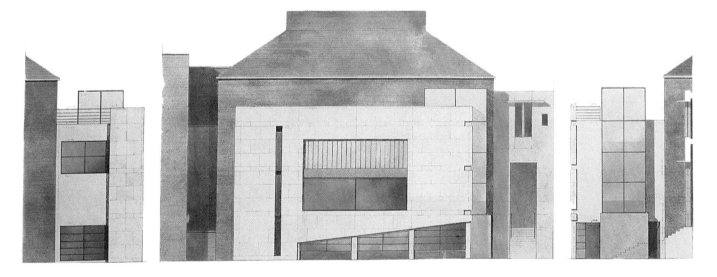

GAIETY SCHOOL OF ACTING

GROUP 91 / PAUL KEOGH ARCHITECTS

The mixed-use building which houses the Gaiety School of Acting forms the west side of Meeting House Square, and rebuilds a long-derelict stretch of Sycamore Street.

The form of the building arises out of specific responses to the existing built fabric and Meeting House Square. In particular, the west side of the square has been designed in response to four principal determinants:

- the new enclosure of Meeting House Square, including the preservation of the existing brick building on the north-west corner of the square
- the patterns of new east-west and north-south pedestrian routes through the square
- the improvement of the environment of Sycamore Street

- the desire to animate the urban space and intensify ground-floor uses in general.

The Gaiety School of Acting occupies the top two floors of the building. The rehearsal studios are large and address the square, while the offices are kept to a minimum and address the street. The office walls curve to introduce movement of space in the entrance area. Showers and changing rooms are confined to the stone service tower. On the top floor, a double-height space is made to allow for juggling, improvisation and dance.

PAUL KEOGH
Architects

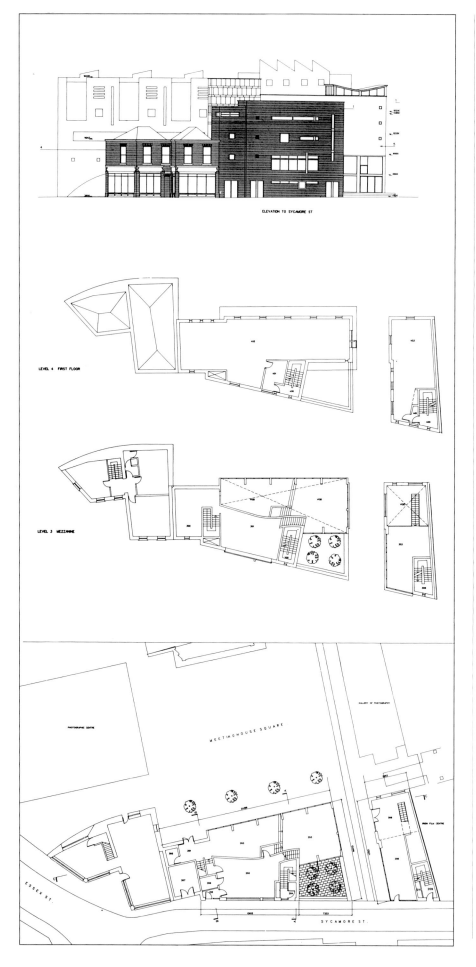

ELEVATION TO SYCAMORE ST

LEVEL 4 FIRST FLOOR

LEVEL 3 MEZZANINE

The Gaiety School of Acting – founded by Joe Dowling in 1986 – came to view its new home in early 1995. It was then an empty shell, standing in a prime location on one of the four sides of Meeting House Square at the very heart of cultural Temple Bar.

Working closely with the architects, we created an optimum use of space. The internal fit-out gave us three well-lit studios – two with durable lino, one with a sprung dance floor – a student meeting area, a meeting/reading room, showers, toilets, a reception area, storage and three offices.

In January 1996 we opened for business in Temple Bar. The building has been an unqualified success. Rigid time and space management have ensured that all our courses are catered for. Our end-users, the general public, work well in the building. Soundproofing of walls and doors enable us to have four different activities going on at any one time. Throughout the day, our full-time acting students use every inch available. At night our part-time students attend classes. At weekends our Youth Theatre and Young Gaiety students take classes, while at other times theatre companies use our resources for auditions and readings.

With Meeting House Square coming alive and Sycamore Street being brightened, our location is perfect. To me, as a user, the spaces in the building are ideal. They provide a creatively conducive environment in which the function of the space is fulfilled. The work is getting done and the sense of well being at the heart of something essential is present. Being hemmed in by The Ark, the Irish Film Centre and the Photography Centre is an inspiration. We feel that our classes, workshops and lectures will also serve as an inspiration to our colleagues in the square and, indeed, beyond.

Patrick Sutton
Executive Director
May, 1996

ARTHOUSE

GROUP 91 / SHAY CLEARY ARCHITECTS

Arthouse is a four-storey-over-basement building, incorporating exhibition/installation/performance space, multi-media production facilities, an advanced technology library and networked information resources, seminar/meeting rooms, training and development facilities, administration offices for a variety of cultural uses, an Internet café, and two retail units.

In urban design terms, the project forms the south side of the new Curved Street between Temple Lane and Eustace Street. It has a more transparent centre, corresponding to the void of the city block, and allows south light to penetrate through the façade to the new street. This central space takes the form of a raised top-lit atrium which becomes the focus of the building and which can be opened on to the street for special events or performances.

In architectural terms, the project is a volumetrically connected series of spaces from basement to third floor. The main façade, with its random pattern of fenestration, highlights the concave space-making quality of the surface. Like the Temple Bar Music Centre, which forms a corresponding convex curve on the other side of the street, the form of the building and the plan of the street is derived from a wish to capitalise on dereliction as an opportunity to create public space, to integrate existing structures into new buildings and to create a new and vivid reality out of the interaction between new interventions and existing circumstances.

The existing narrow frontage house at No.22 Eustace Street is integrated into the project and provides a powerful contrast at close quarters between old and new. Spatially, . the building is planned in an open manner with an interlocking series of large volumes, which form a route through the building. The smaller offices and meeting areas are positioned discretely around this larger arrangement. Generally the project has a strong visual connection to the street, both at ground and first floor, where the larger, more public spaces are located.

The architectural potential of the concave façade to the new street is exploited to the full through the use of a smooth render finish and by the composition of the openings. The elevations to Temple Lane and Eustace Street refer, in a non-literal way, through their scale and appearance, to a quasi-industrial and a townhouse aesthetic respectively.

SHAY CLEARY Architects

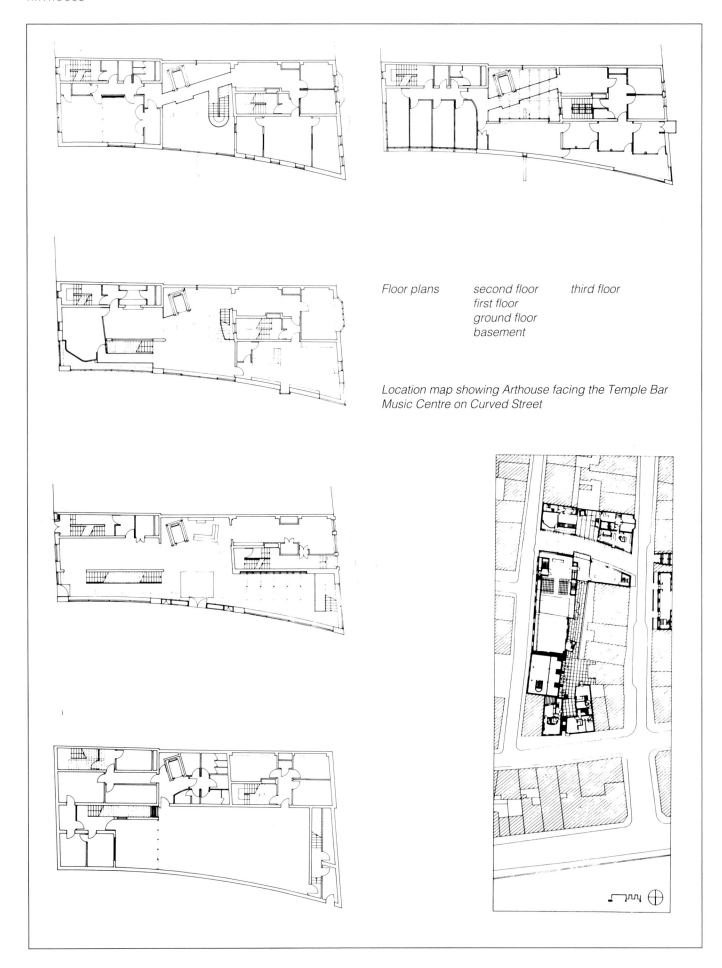

Floor plans   second floor   third floor
first floor
ground floor
basement

Location map showing Arthouse facing the Temple Bar Music Centre on Curved Street

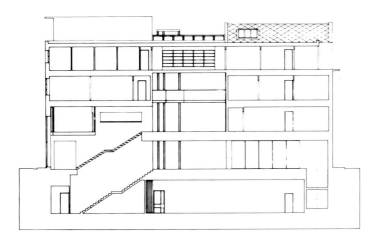

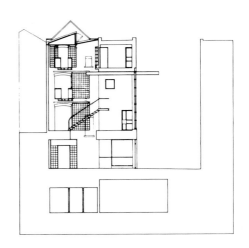

Perspective view of Arthouse, looking west

top – Cyberia café at the Temple Lane end of Arthouse

bottom – *The Eustace Street end of Arthouse showing No.22 which was refurbished and integrated into the project*

opposite

Views of the first-floor café and the double-height window onto Curved Street

Arthouse, the multi-media centre for the arts, is one of the new initiatives undertaken by Temple Bar Properties as part of its mission to develop the Cultural Quarter. It is one of the first purpose-built multi-media centres for the arts in the world. When I joined Temple Bar Properties in 1992 to develop the concept for a centre that would provide a multi-media laboratory for the arts, there were no models elsewhere that encompassed training, production, exhibition and promotion facilities for the creative community in one integrated programme supported by new technology. Because of this, and the fact that computers were not yet widely seen as creative tools, the evolution of both the concept and the building were very closely intertwined.

The demands of an evolving brief initially placed some creative strains on the client/architect relationship – designing for an evolving concept was never going to be a straightforward brief. We were many months into the design of the centre before we both fully grasped the nature and ambition of the project. However, when we did, a very rich collaboration commenced. The architect was unstinting in his determination to address the complexity of designing the multi-media centre, and has delivered a building in which versatility is a key component.

Now, as an end-user of this arts centre, I ask myself did all the thoughtful research and consultation deliver a building that works. The honest answer is, I still do not know. This is a building designed to function across a broad agenda that is still largely untested. In the past six months, since moving into the new centre, the company has been building up its programme of activities and has been testing its technical backbone. The architect has provided us with an imaginative building that certainly accommodates the distinct units and functions of the Arthouse programme. Although it is still early days, for its current daily end-users Arthouse is a fabulous building in which to work.

Arthouse is a building with a heart. Cyberia (the Internet café) is situated in the raised atrium court on the first floor. The atrium forms the heart of the building from which all arteries flow, by way of the glazed metal walkways, to the upper- second- and third-floor rooms. The ground-floor reception and exhibition space are completely transparent to the street, providing an excellent shop window to present new media work to the public. A sixteen-monitor video wall at the main entrance is proving to be a popular exhibition site.

It is a bright, open, airy building with many thoughtful design features – unusual wall curves, overhanging rooms and internal windows that open up surprising views through the building. Its clean lines and minimalist use of materials and colour might announce the high-tech functionality of the building, but the great technical capacity of Arthouse is hidden in its cabling and trunking systems. The forty kilometres of cabling make it capable of handling the advanced communications systems that will enable Irish artists to explore the creative capacity of new computer technology, and network with the world.

Arthouse and the Temple Bar Music Centre have incorporated a number of features on the façades of the buildings to support the future use of Curved Street as a special public event space. Both buildings have rails to carry external lighting rigs and to support a roof-top canopy to cover the street. With full services to the street, including computerised control of audio, video and lighting systems, Curved Street offers much potential for performance events. This infrastructure is a consequence of the integrated public art policy Temple Bar Properties brought to the development of the Cultural Quarter. Although it will take time to utilise and programme the space, a major focus of the design brief was to build not just for today, but for the future as well.

Aileen MacKeogh
Director
May 1996

Broadcasting live from the basement performance space in Arthouse

TEMPLE BAR MUSIC CENTRE

GROUP 91 / McCULLOUGH MULVIN ARCHITECTS

The Temple Bar Music Centre is a four-storey-over-basement building containing an auditorium, music rehearsal rooms, music information facilities and teaching areas. The Curved Street project, of which the Music Centre forms one half, is an important part of the urban regeneration of the quarter, in helping to establish the east-west route from Temple Bar Square to Meeting House Square. The curved shape of the street was at least partly derived from a desire to avoid removing existing buildings – the route is a careful line using derelict space to best advantage.

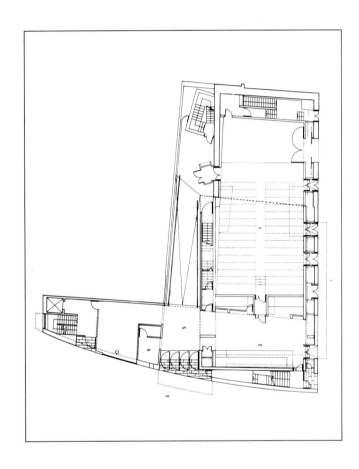

In addition to its modern façade on Curved Street, the building includes the substance of two warehouses on Temple Lane, and has a presence on Eustace Street as a narrow, contemporary elevation beside the 18th-century townhouse at No.18. Site boundaries were given elements in the overall design of the building: one side curved, the rest an irregular edge dictated by existing buildings. The geometry of the plan reflects the juxtaposition of necessary angles. In the interests of conservation, most of the existing 19th-century warehouses at No.11 and the façade at No.10 Temple Lane were retained. No.10 had been substantially rebuilt in the 1930s.

The brief for the Temple Bar Music Centre grew out of a set of indigenous Temple Bar cultural uses – training rooms, music rehearsal rooms, offices for music-related activities – mostly based in existing but semi-derelict warehouses within CIÉ's bus station site. This brief was complemented by the addition of a music venue for 350 people, with ancillary bar and service areas. Such disparate uses with conflicting requirements for sound and silence had to be housed in a relatively small space between existing buildings. Thus, the requirements for acoustic insulation of various kinds – between different parts of the buildings and between the Music Centre and its neighbours – has influenced the design of the building from the start, giving a relatively closed architecture of box-in-box construction, with layers of isolation between sound sources.

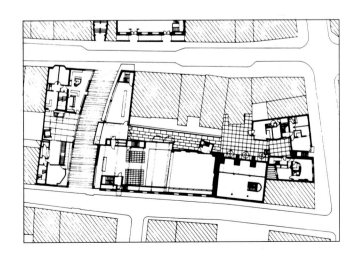

Architecturally, the scheme is a dialogue of objects hidden and revealed behind screens as the observer moves around and through the building. The screens are the façade of Curved Street (a plain render and stone façade with one

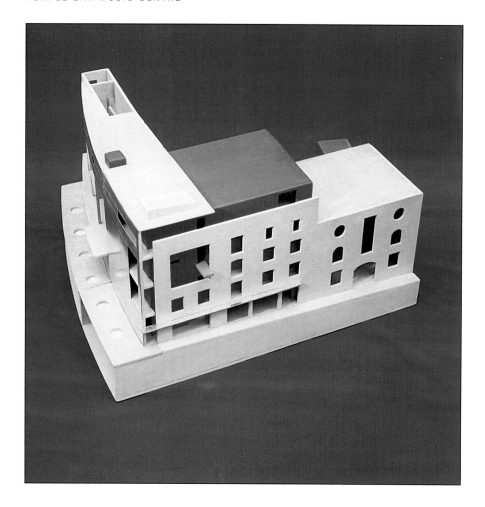

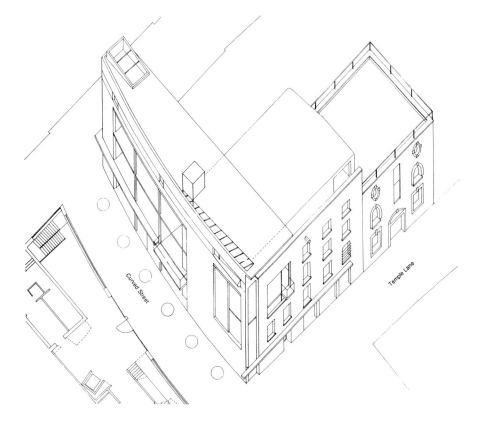

dramatic glazed opening) and the retained elements of Nos.10 and 11 Temple Lane (traditional façades with small regular openings). They shield a 'black box' containing the auditorium behind the façade of 10 Temple Lane, aspects of which appear and disappear at different angles – a scheme in the traditional manner of an 18th-century Dublin Dissenter meeting house or chapel, hidden in the centre of a block. The Temple Lane/Curved Street corner is dominated by a vertical cut, revealing a roof-lit staircase trapped between the box and the curved wall, which serves as an introduction to the urban design sequence from Temple Bar Square in the traditional heart of Temple Bar, through Curved Street to Meeting House Square beyond.

The main entrance on Curved Street – marked by a projecting balcony – runs into a long, yellow foyer, pinned by a silver staircase tower at the end. The upper level of this provides a raised open courtyard that runs between the building on both sides. Street and courtyard are linked by a double-height space.

The Temple Bar Music Centre relates to the existing built fabric without reproducing it. Its architecture derives from a merging of old and new, the old transformed, remodelled and counter-pointed with clearly modern elements, both aspects gaining by juxtaposition with one another.

The Temple Bar Music Centre opened in May 1996.

McCULLOUGH MULVIN
Architects

———

Model of the Temple Bar Music Centre
Axonometric drawing

opposite
top left – Main entrance
*top right –*View from top of stairs
Perspective view of the building

DUBLIN'S VIKING ADVENTURE

GILROY McMAHON ARCHITECTS

This ensemble of buildings was acquired by Temple Bar Properties in 1991. Its use as a Viking centre had been identified in Dublin Corporation's Dublin City Area Development Plan as a strategic development which was seen as providing a catalyst for stimulating change on the very derelict sites along the backbone of Temple Bar.

The brief was to provide a variety of accommodation containing formal and interactive exhibition spaces, which would be linked through the existing buildings in a specific circulation sequence. The spaces had to incorporate air conditioning, security and communication systems, and allow for flexibility for changing exhibitions in the future.

The starting point for the design was to be a combination of the brief, the existing buildings themselves, and their unique history. In addition, the buildings had a previous functional relationship as a church, schoolhouse and community hall. All were still physically intact, but in a very bad state of disrepair.

The buildings were constructed on the foundations of surface medieval structures, and the former church of SS Michael & John had been installed within the shell of the mid-17th-century Smock Alley Theatre. It was discovered that there were important traces of all these different interventions into these buildings over the years, and the design team determined that the story of the history of these buildings should be allowed to tell itself through the exposed features in the final design.

The architectural approach of the project was to seek an integration of this programme and make it compatible with the existing context, function and legibility. The architects have, therefore, conceived the project as a 'suspended museum' contained within the restored fabric of the existing buildings, to allow the public to experience history as the presence of the past brought alive by archaeology. They have attempted to find a new relationship between these distinct individual buildings and the objects that they will contain. The buildings should be enjoyed physically through movement as much as visually, as visitors explore what is an interpretation of selected aspects of this place.

Two important factors emerged in the final design. One was that any intervention should be clearly seen for what it is and viewed separately from the existing building. The other was that any interventions into these existing buildings would be treated as an installation and must be capable of being removed and the space restored at a later date to the original state. Indeed, the whole design approach was intentionally flexible to allow the spaces to be used in a variety of ways, both now and in the future.

GILROY McMAHON Architects

Elevation to Essex Street West

opposite
View along Essex Street, with the new
Civic Offices in the background

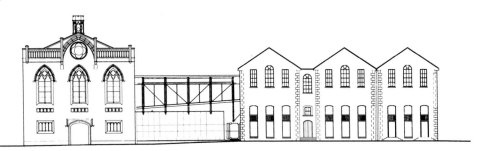

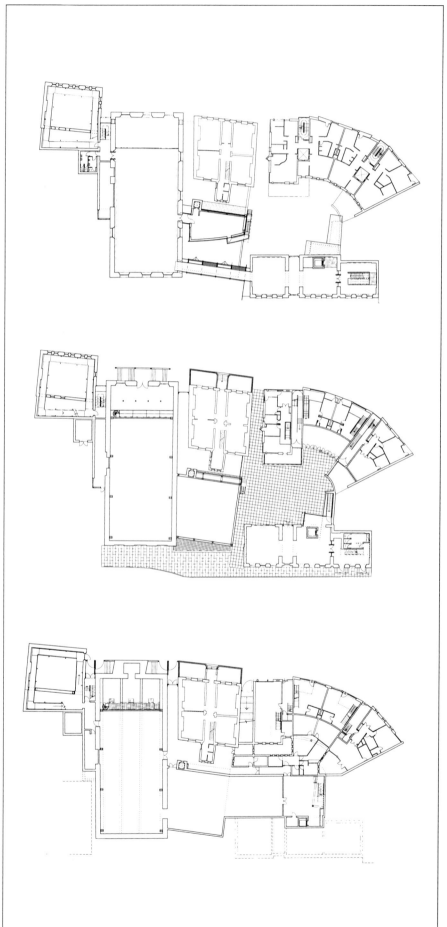

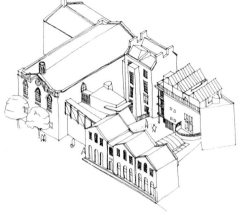

*Birdseye sketch of the complex
comprising a former church,
schoolhouse and community hall*

*Plans   first floor
            ground floor
            lower ground floor*

opposite

*Views of the entrance courtyard with
sculptural wall by Grace Weir*

NATIONAL PHOTOGRAPHY ARCHIVE / DIT SCHOOL OF PHOTOGRAPHY

GROUP 91 / O'DONNELL AND TUOMEY ARCHITECTS

NATIONAL PHOTOGRAPHY CENTRE

Two buildings with a mixture of photography uses face each other across Meeting House Square, linked by moving and still images projected from the archive building on to the screen window of the gallery.

The building complex brings together varied but related aspects of photographic culture. It is designed to accommodate the identity of each of the constituent parts, and to allow for overlap and cross-contact between photographs as social document and historical record, the education and training of photographers, and the art and practice of contemporary photography.

NATIONAL PHOTOGRAPHY ARCHIVE / DIT SCHOOL

The archive and school are housed in a five-storey-over-basement brick building on the north side of Meeting House Square. The brief called for the exclusion of daylight from studios, darkrooms, lecture rooms, archive storage and exhibition areas. The pivotal location of the building within Temple Bar suggested the need for a strong architectural presence. The building is faced in brick, with small-scale repetitive elements forming a consistent visual rhythm, with larger scale elements identifying the special character of its public use.

The arched form of the building is intended to make a formal entry from the forecourt to the National Photography Archive, as well as making a visual link between Essex Street East and Meeting House Square by 'bridging the gap'.

The archives and photographic services are contained in an air-conditioned basement, where humidity and temperature are carefully controlled to create optimum conditions for the storage of up to a quarter of a million glass-plate negatives. Public entry to the galleries, reference room and bookshop is from the limestone forecourt over the archive basement.

The DIT School of Photography has its own entrance from Essex Street East, with stair and lift to second-floor offices, darkrooms and teaching spaces, and with double-height studio and darkroom units at top floor, overlooking the street, square and city skyline. The upper-level studios of the DIT School of Photography are expressed as a series of smaller units, making a broken skyline related to the scale of the warehouses in Temple Bar.

The National Photography Archive / DIT School of Photography was completed in June 1996.

O'DONNELL AND TUOMEY
Architects

Section through the Photography Centre buildings on Meeting House Square

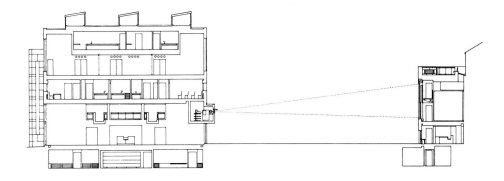

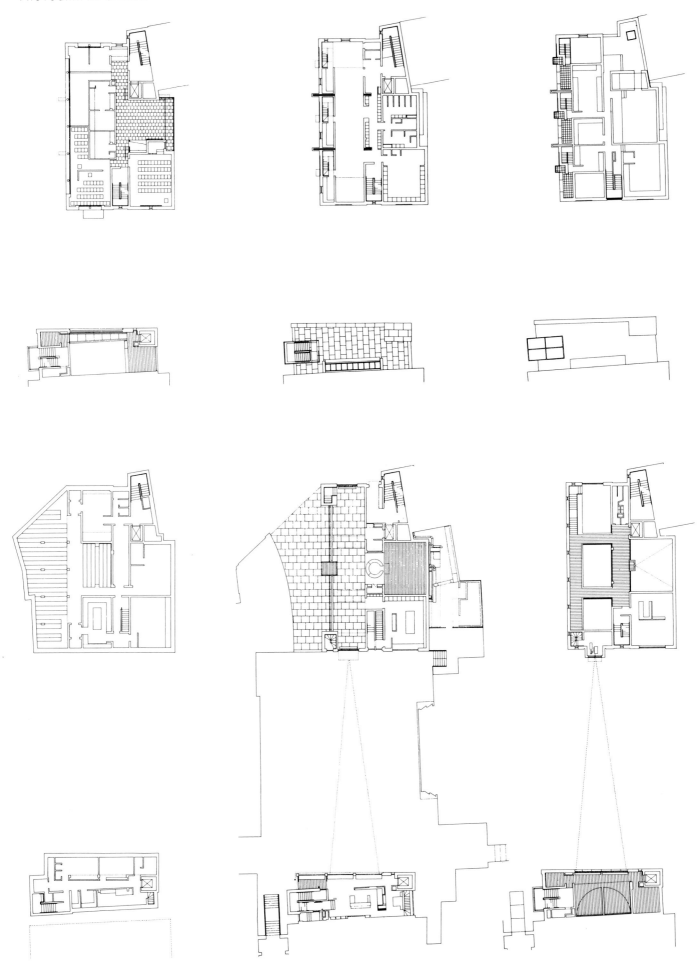

Inaugural film show in Meeting House
Square, June 1996

opposite

Floor plans of the Photography Centre
(Archive / DIT building at top,
Gallery of Photography at bottom):

2nd floor	3rd floor	4th floor
basement	ground floor	1st floor

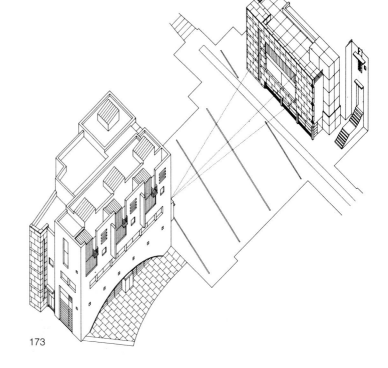

173

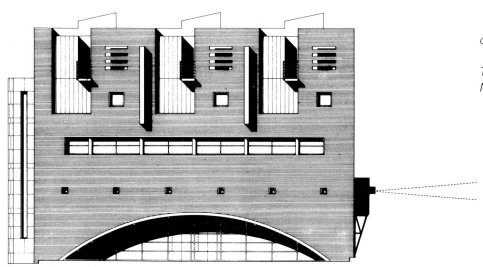

The building nears completion

opposite

The arched entrance and foyer of the National Photography Archive

PROJECT ARTS CENTRE

SHAY CLEARY ARCHITECTS

Project Arts Centre is celebrating its thirtieth birthday in 1996. After several temporary homes – including an engineering premises in Lower Abbey Street and a disused clothing factory in South King Street – Project moved to its present location in Essex Street East in 1974. After the Olympia Theatre, it is the oldest cultural organisation in the Temple Bar area and is one of Ireland's leading arts centres. Its primary objective is to present and promote work which is new and innovative and serves all art forms.

Within the envelope of this industrial premises, you will find a theatre, two visual arts spaces and ancillary facilities. The external fabric was maintained down through the years, and internal refurbishment was undertaken from time to time.

The condition of the original building has now deteriorated to such an extent that substantial work would be required to bring it up to a satisfactory level. Project Arts Centre is working alongside Temple Bar Properties to formulate a scheme of development for a new arts centre, in the same location, incorporating and expanding on its existing facilities: performance spaces, a visual arts space, with ancillary activity and service areas, including front-of-house facilities. Shay Cleary Architects has been retained by Temple Bar Properties to lead the design team for the project, for which it is intended that a planning application will be lodged in the summer of 1996.

FIACH MAC CONGHAIL
Director
May, 1996

Case Studies

INTRODUCTION

FOUR SCHEMES OF DEVELOPMENT HAVE BEEN DESCRIBED IN some detail to illustrate three of the guiding principles of the Temple Bar project: innovation; the reuse of existing fabric and the maximisation of gap sites; and the development of exemplary mixed-use residential/retail projects – what is described as 'Living Over The Shop'. The case-study examples also give some insight into the development approach and the factors which influenced design decisions. The buildings selected – Nos.17 and 18 Eustace Street, the Green Building, and The Printworks – all illustrate in their own way the sequence of feasibility assessment, development of brief and design/development processes which go into a building project, whether it is reusing or restoring existing fabric, as in the case of the first two; a mixture of old and new, in the case of the third; or an entirely new building, in the fourth.

The descriptions of Nos.17 and 18 Eustace Street elaborate, with reference to two specific projects, the complex language of preservation, restoration and conservation, and the background to the complex process of reusing old building fabric in the context of contemporary standards, regulations, and building uses. The Green Building treats existing regulations and technologies as a departure point, and represents a living, working demonstration of the potential for 'green' architecture to have a radical impact on the technology of building design and construction in the 21st century. The Printworks represents an example of the kind of mixture of uses – public/commercial and private/residential – which form an essential component of the urban framework plan.

PQ

Case Studies

THE PRINTWORKS

GROUP 91 / DEREK TYNAN ARCHITECTS

THIS PROJECT, CONSISTING OF TEN APARTMENTS AND FOUR studio/retail units, was one of the first mixed-use developments to be completed under the urban framework plan, and was intended to develop certain principles of the plan – notably, the creative use of existing buildings and gap sites to provide a significant increase in the resident population. The model of the raised court, as a sectional means of reinhabiting the upper floors of the city fabric, was proposed to adapt the characteristically narrow blocks for this intensification of residential use, while nonetheless exploiting more commercial ground-floor space for retail purposes.

The site for the project is an L-shaped section of the Temple Lane / Eustace Street block, with frontage on to Temple Lane. The block has been developed to the south by the Music Centre, facing on to the new Curved Street. The principal frontage of the project is on to Essex Street East, which is hierarchically important as the principal east/west route through Temple Bar. Elements to be retained on the site were the existing two-storey, early 20th-century façade on Temple Lane, and the majority of the 18th-century building forming part of the frontage on to Essex Street itself. A gap site one plot wide formed the remainder of the portfolio of individual properties to be developed under this scheme.

The development strategy which informed the brief for the project was to accept and exploit the configurational and sectional diversity of the retained elements, and through a complementary process of adaptation, insertion and new construction, to form a prototypical urban type – the raised court. Below the new site, created by the construction of this podium level, a series of independent shops and commercial uses can exploit the street frontage. Above, the interior of the block is transformed into a semi-public space, with the court mediating between the three different buildings and providing access to a total of ten apartments. The apartments themselves are designed with specific reference to the surrounding streets and the raised court, creating a catalogue of dwelling types which demonstrate the potential of urban living.

For the purpose of description, the development can be analysed in terms of its three component elements:

25 ESSEX STREET EAST

The brief required this four-storey, late Georgian building to be retained, as it originally formed part of a terrace of which itself and the adjoining property to the east are the only remaining buildings. The building had, however, not been used for some time, the original stairway had been removed, and the rear section had significant structural difficulties and dry rot. Nonetheless, it was possible to retain the existing floors, walls and windows.

The strategy was to retain the existing shell of the building, and within it to insert three apartments. Access to the apartments is from the lower level of the raised court, allowing a commercial use to occupy all of the ground floor. At first- and second-floor levels are single-bedroom apartments, with kitchens and bathrooms designed as an inserted object in the centre of the plan. At third-floor and roof level is a large duplex apartment, incorporating the stairway from the second floor, third-floor kitchen, living and bedroom spaces, and an upper mezzanine connecting to a south-facing roof garden. This apartment has the benefit of a private roof garden.

26 & 27 ESSEX STREET EAST

The new infill building forms retail units at ground-floor level, with four apartments above. The three single-storey apartments on the street-frontage building overlook the street, and have through living rooms facing south on to the raised courtyard. In order to continue the fenestration pattern of the adjoining building, the floor levels are aligned, leading to a varied section height – the lower levels having the advantage of higher ceilings, the uppermost apartment exploiting the roof profile and incorporating south-facing roof lights to compensate for the lower ceiling height at the street elevation. These apartments share a roof garden, accessed from the entrance stairway, which becomes one of a series of roof gardens developed in the project and in other nearby developments (such as the Temple Bar Music Centre), providing a new series of public and private spaces at roof level in Temple Bar.

Within the raised court, a duplex apartment is 'hidden' within

the block, with no street frontage. It has a large living space, characterised by the opaque glass box to the courtyard which admits light but protects privacy, and a roof garden at upper level. Together, these form an apartment with a particular reclusive quality.

12 & 13 TEMPLE LANE

The brief required the existing 20th-century façade, previously the printworks from which the project derives its commercial name, to be retained, both as a piece of industrial architecture and as a talisman within the popular consciousness of the area. As the existing buildings were derelict, a new four-storey building was constructed behind the façade on an independent structure, consisting of a two-storey studio space on the lower floors, with apartments above.

The studio was subsequently fitted out as the design studio of the fashion designer John Rocha. His brief was to accommodate design functions, periodic display collections and offices, with actual production and retailing taking place elsewhere. The two floors are linked by double-height spaces over the pattern room and reception areas, allowing the various activities to be visually connected.

Three studio-type duplex apartments, which are entered by a stairs ascending from the raised court, have been set back from the retained façade at third-floor level. These apartments have double-height living spaces with bedroom galleries, lit from south-facing clerestory lights and two roof terraces, which are generated from the set-back over the existing façade.

DEREK TYNAN
Architect

top – Raised courtyard and entry from Essex Street

bottom – Temple Lane – the former printworks is now a two-storey design studio, with apartments above

opposite

top – The brick façade to Essex Street East

*bottom – Ground and 1st floor plans
(2nd and 3rd floor plans overleaf)*

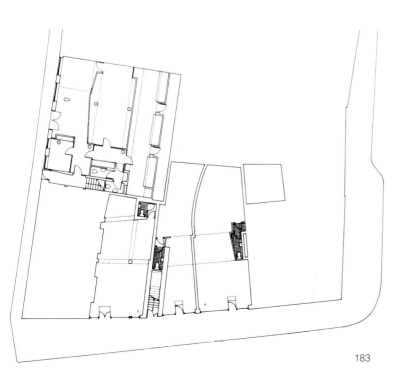

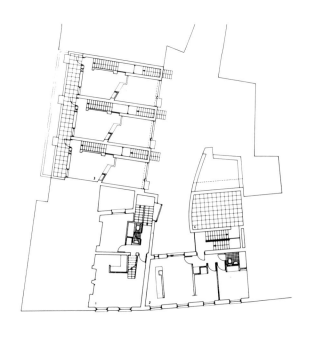

opposite and above
Ground-floor retail and studio spaces in the Printworks

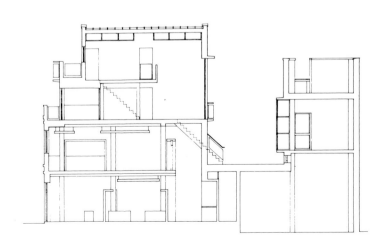

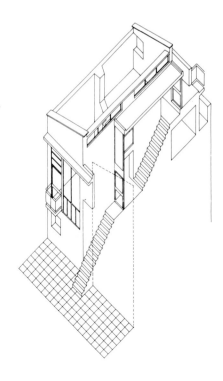

THE GREEN BUILDING

MURRAY O'LAOIRE ASSOCIATES, ARCHITECTS

THE GREEN BUILDING, LOCATED ON TWO SUBSTANTIAL GAP sites on Temple Lane South and Crow Street, has its origin in a speculative 'generic' proposal to the EU Thermie Programme in 1990. The proposing group, inter-alia, included the architects, Tim Cooper, Director of Buildings, Trinity College Dublin, and Owen Lewis, Director of the Energy Research Group at University College Dublin. The proposal was given in-principle support by the European Commission, subject to the proposers finding a suitable site and a sympathetic developer. In 1992, Temple Bar Properties undertook to develop the project, subject to the EU's continuing support for the principles of the project on a site which demanded a considerably different response than that envisaged in the 'generic' proposal (which assumed, for example, optimal orientation on three façades – a condition not present on the Crow Street / Temple Lane site).

This fortunate metamorphosis, induced in the first instance by site context and not insignificantly by Temple Bar Properties' desire to develop a building of mixed-used composition (consistent with its redevelopment strategy), resulted in a brief which is in many ways more relevant as a European prototype than the building originally envisaged. Temple Bar Properties also saw the project as a reference and benchmark for its own energy philosophy in respect of the redevelopment of this historic area of Dublin.

It is important to state the while EU funding through the Thermie Programme was secured, this was confined to support research and monitoring of the 'demonstration' elements of the project. The 'green' technologies of which the Green Building is such a rich and diverse example are not so much new as untested in a commercial environment. The purpose of the Thermie grant, therefore, was to produce a building that would be commercially viable and whose design philosophy and demonstrably energy-efficient performance would therefore be transferable throughout the EU.

The building had therefore to possess both 'archetypal' and 'prototypical' attributes; 'archetypal' in the sense that its use and composition would respect broadly those associated with historic European urban centres; and prototypical in the sense that it would be among a handful of such projects which sought to stimulate, provoke and direct the design of

The two façades of the Green Building – Crow Street (above) and Temple Lane (opposite)

buildings in similar circumstances into the new century, in an accessible and commercially viable manner.

Notwithstanding the polemical purpose of the project, both client and architect were mindful from the outset to avoid the creation of a 'freak', and to produce a building derived from the primary eternal generators of architecture: space, light and climate. This building is, therefore, ultimately about balances. It does not set out to maximise any one design parameter. The image of an introverted massive building with minimum window apertures proclaiming only energy efficiency was dismissed in favour of total and balanced exploration of the architectural potential of bio-climatic principles. While the use of recycled and environmentally friendly materials is fundamental to the project, the architects were concerned to go beyond tokenism in the integration of art and craft elements in the building.

Building Layout

The site is a 26m-long double plot with 11m east- and west-facing frontages on Crow Street and Temple Lane. The building is laid out around a six-storey central courtyard, which is oriented southwards and designed to give natural ventilation and light to the building. Temple Lane and Crow Street are narrow streets, approximately 5-6 metres wide, with four-storey buildings on either side, where the amount of natural light is minimal. The brief for the building determined that there should be commercial uses (retail and office) at ground and basement levels, and eight apartments on the upper three levels.

The Courtyard

The courtyard is designed as a semi-external space, with the commercial and residential units having access to it for lighting and ventilation. The glazed, opening roof is designed to have a fail-safe opening clear area, equal to the plan area of the floor void for smoke venting. Thus, the courtyard is classed as an external space, allowing non-fire-rated opening windows facing into the space. At ground and basement level, a pool humidifies the air and provides acoustic 'white' noise. At first-floor level, the courtyard has an inclined glazed screen, maximising the availability of natural light. Glass-block galleries at upper levels give access to the apartments, and are hung with dense planting which re-oxygenates the air in the courtyard in winter time. A free-standing steel structure at the southern edge of the courtyard contains the lift. The structure is designed to allow maximum light penetration into the courtyard. This structure is clad in glass at lower levels, with the lift mechanism exposed above.

Elevations

The ground and first-floor elevation is expressed as one volume, giving scale and presence on the street, with four recessed bays, each bay treated differently, responding to the functions behind. The bays contain shop entrances, dis-

play units, a ventilation duct which affords a view to the basement garden and doors giving access to upper floors, designed and manufactured to architects' and engineers' specifications, but clad in recycled materials by the two artists concerned. At the upper levels, where greater amounts of natural light is available, window-to-wall area is reduced, incorporating bay windows/window gardens, revolving windows and balcony planters. The walls are of massive construction, highly insulated with rock wool insulation, and finished with a coloured plaster render. Trellis wires provide support for external planting. The fourth floor is set back, clad in copper, affording roof-level balconies to the three-bedroom apartments. The copper-clad roof with wind turbines, solar panels and opening roof provide unique vistas to the surrounding streets and further afield.

Materials

In order to minimise environmental impact, materials selected for use in the building were analysed in terms of raw material, manufacturing process, embodied energy, installation and life cycle, recyclability/bio-degradability. For example, the windows in the building are softwood from managed renewable plantations, with water-based, solvent-free paint finishes. Floor finishes are linoleum and natural jute carpets. Kitchens are made from recycled pitch pine and recycled terracotta tiles, and so on. There are some materials used in the building for which there were no 'green' alternatives; for example, it was not possible to source recycled aggregate for the concrete locally, nor was it possible to use recycled copper for the roof, as was originally envisaged. The amount of steel used in the building is kept to a minimum and used for its functional performance only.

Many elements of the fabric of the building which would normally be carried out by the main contractor were designed and installed by artists/artisans. The entrance panels at Crow Street and Temple Lane are supplied by Remco de Fouw and Maud Cotter; recycled bicycle balustrades are by James Garner; the atrium duct is by Vivienne Roche; light fittings, bathroom fittings and bicycle stands are supplied by Brian McDonald; kitchens by Tadgh O'Driscoll, and hand-painted tiles are provided by the Tileworks.

Energy Efficiency

Since the mid-1980s, annual energy consumption in modern office buildings in Dublin has risen to somewhere in the order of 175m kilowatt hours annually, and currently energy consumed in modern offices in Dublin alone results in annual emissions of over 95,000 tonnes of CO_2. The modern building industry has had a major impact on the natural CO_2 balance in three ways. Firstly, it has placed huge demand on the system by purchasing large quantities of timber for use during construction and this has led to the destruction of forests which have played a vital role in maintaining the natural CO_2 balance. Secondly, large quantities of CO_2 are emitted during many of the manufacturing process involved in the

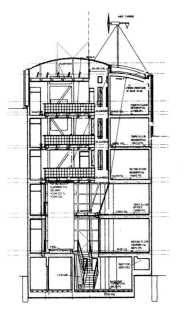

above – The atrium

left – Short section through the atrium

right – Long section from Temple Lane to Crow Street

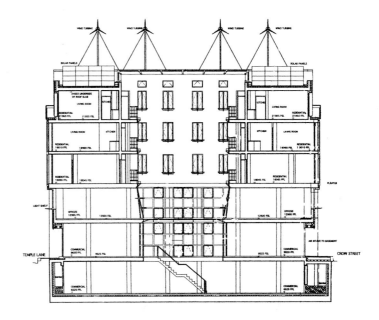

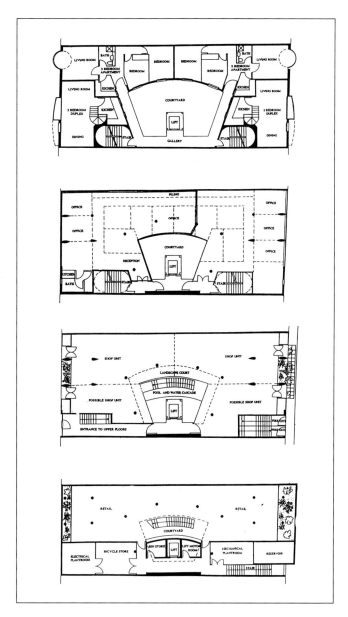

Basement, ground, 1st and 3rd floor plans

refinement and production of materials and components for the building industry. Thirdly, the consumption of energy when the building is in use results in continuous emissions of large quantities of CO_2 and other so-called 'greenhouse' gases, throughout the life of the building.

The design of the Green Building addresses the issue of energy use and CO_2 emissions in the following ways:
• The building is constructed in massive form to prevent it being effected by short-term variations in weather conditions, and encased in an insulated cover to minimise heat loss through its fabric.
• In summer, ventilation air enters a large chamber at basement level and is filtered and conditioned naturally, passing through dense planting. Air passes from this chamber to the central courtyard, which again contains extensive areas of specially selected planting, which then passes out through the opening roof by way of the stack effect.

• In winter, the roof remains closed, air at high level is pre-heated and mixed with small amounts of fresh air which is naturally pre-heated by way of a natural heat exchanger, and re-circulated down to low level in the courtyard by way of the fabric duct.

Heating and cooling

A heat pump connected to a specially constructed 150m-deep well provides hot water at night – using low-cost electricity – to a thermal reservoir at basement level, where it is stored for release during the day. The energy stored in the reservoir is distributed through the building structure through pipes embedded in the concrete floors and ceilings.

The electric lights use advanced energy-efficient technologies designed to complement daylighting. High-frequency fluorescent lamps will provide background illumination of 160 lux. Higher levels of work-surface lighting will be achieved by use of high-efficiency task lighting. Electricity used to power the lighting systems will be drawn from lead-acid batteries, charged by the rooftop solar photovoltaic panels and wind generators. These batteries are also used to provide stand-by power for the fire escape ventilation system.

Thirty percent window-to-wall areas are used to optimise solar gain/heat loss ratios and daylighting. The windows are very high quality – double-glazed, argon-filled units in timber frames, designed to minimise thermal bridging.

From an energy efficiency point of view, the whole building has been modelled using a state-of-the-art computer simulation called ESP+, located in Dublin and Scotland. This simulation enables the designers to evaluate rapidly and accurately the performance of the building (air temperature, air movement, relatively humidity and lighting levels) in just about every conceivable circumstance. It provides the design engineers with a hitherto unavailable depth of diagnostic analysis that allows repeated detailed investigation of every aspect of the design. Preliminary design studies have indicated that the annual energy consumption of this building would be 80% less than that of a conventional building.

Conclusion

Notwithstanding many of its prototypical attributes, it is hoped that this building will be seen ultimately as an 'ordinary' building. In addition to demonstrating the accessibility of bio-climatic design principles, the objective has been to develop a transferable building type, housing a range of user groups. This heterogeneity and pluralism is often aspired to but rarely achieved. The coexistence of the parts will be interesting to observe and monitor, as will the environment design performance of the building over time.

MURRAY O'LAOIRE
Architects

17 & 18 EUSTACE STREET

INTRODUCTION

URING THE LATTER HALF OF THE 16TH CENTURY, FOLLOWing the suppression of the monasteries by Henry VIII, the monastic lands and estates to the east of the old medieval city of Dublin were transferred to private ownership or held as public lands by the city. The Liberties of St Thomas and Donore were vested in William Brabazon); the lands of St Mary's were purchased by the Moore family; the properties of the Monastery of All Saints were given to the 'New University' of Dublin (Trinity College), which was established in 1592; the Aungier family acquired the property of the Carmelites (the Whitefriars); iIn the area now known as Temple Bar, the Crowe family took possession of the lands of the Augustinian monastery.

Large mansions were erected on these 'Temple Bar' properties, and, accordingly, the area became one of high fashion. These houses, along present-day College Green, Dame Street, etc, were described as 'substantial', with gardens running northwards down to the River Liffey. Families whose names are still connected with the area – the Crowes, the Eustaces, the Angleseas and the Temples – all lived in what is now known as Temple Bar. The outlines of the gardens of their houses would greatly influence planning of the area when it was more extensively developed in the 17th and 18th centuries, and, indeed, has influenced the layout of the area right up to the present day.

Following the restoration of the monarchy in 1660, and in particular with the appointment of James, Duke of Ormonde, as Viceroy, the pattern of the modern city of Dublin was established. Increased prosperity and pressure of business during the 17th century resulted in the erection of the quay wall along the low-water tide-line and the reclaiming of the lands to the south of it. This more or less increased the land area of Temple Bar to its current dimensions. The first phase of building on this reclaimed land still saw streets of houses running parallel to the river, with their gardens extending to the new quay wall. However, with the construction of 'the quays', the present regular street plan was established with Essex Street, Temple Bar and Fleet Street forming its spine.

The 'substantial houses' with their gardens, which constituted the first post-monastic building phase, were, by the end of the 17th and the beginning of the 18th century, giving way to more intensive development of narrow streets running south-north from Dame Street to the Essex Street-Temple Bar-Fleet Street spine. These streets were built on the lands and gardens of the former 'substantial houses', and largely took their plan form from them, and, in many cases, their names from the owners, i.e. Eustace Street, Crow Street, Anglesea Street, and, of course, Temple Bar itself. In some cases – Eustace Street, for example – the street was actually owned by the Eustace family.

As far as can be ascertained, most of the early houses and other buildings which have survived in Temple Bar date from the early part of the 18th century to the 1730s. The Presbyterian Meeting House (now The Ark), one of the most distinguished buildings in the area, dates from approximately 1725, whereas it is probable that most of the houses which survive from the early 18th century date from approximately 1730, give or take a few years. There are, however, some exceptions; for instance, it has recently been established that the 17th-century Smock Alley Theatre survives, buried under 19th-century plasterwork, behind the stone façade of the former church of SS Michael & John. But these remains must, until further evidence comes to light, be regarded as exceptional. Buildings in Eustace Street, which is the concern of these notes, date generally from the early 18th century, with some late 18th- and early 19th-century insertions, such as 18 Eustace Street.

The surviving early 18th-century houses could be described as houses of the lower middle class – well-established tradesmen, clerks, shopkeepers, etc. They would have been reasonably prosperous members of their class, people of taste and people conscious of the changing fashions in interior decoration. Such, probably, were the original occupiers of No.17 Eustace Street.

T AUSTIN DUNPHY

———

opposite – No.18 Eustace Street – the restored townhouse (c.1780-1810) which is home to Temple Bar Properties

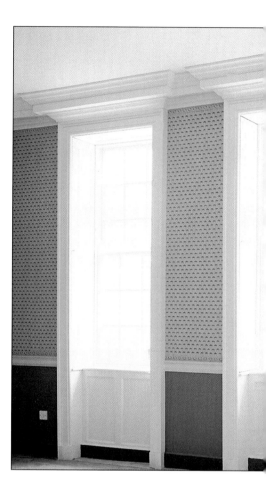

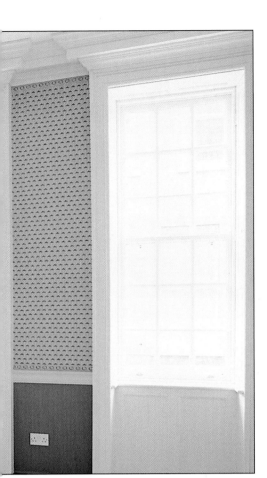

17 EUSTACE STREET

DUNPHY O'CONNOR BAIRD
ARCHITECTS

No.17 EUSTACE STREET WAS AMONGST THE PROPERTIES IN the 'core area' of Temple Bar acquired by Temple Bar Properties from CIÉ in 1991. It is one of a number of broadly similar houses in the street, each about the same size and with many features in common. Many originally had a gable facing on to the street, a simplified form of the famous 'Dutch Billies' – introduced to Dublin at the turn of the 17th and 18th centuries. Examples of this type of house were to be found throughout the Dublin of the late 17th and early 18th centuries, but particularly in the old Huguenot areas such as Weaver Square, Bridgefoot Street, Longford Street, Cork Street, Temple Bar, etc. Unfortunately most of the best examples were destroyed over the years, so that the few which have been left are of great architectural and historic value. It was decided by Temple Bar Properties to commission a comprehensive evaluation of the building, and subsequently to undertake its conservation in full, with the help of a grant from the National Heritage Council.

Philosophy of the Restoration

As can be seen from photographs taken prior to the commencement of the restoration works, the building was in a sorry state. The gable facing the street had been demolished and the entire floor behind it removed. The original pitched roof had been replaced with a flat roof at third-floor level. The original brickwork façade had been plastered over, the top-floor windows built up, the first and second-floor windows greatly altered, and the two ground-floor windows totally removed and replaced by one wide 'shop window'.

Internally, its condition was as bad, if not worse. Many of the floors and parts of the staircase were in a dangerous state, and there was much evidence of low-grade alterations carried out in recent times. However, through all this degradation, one could still see the features of an early 18th-century house. It appeared also that an effort had been made to bring the first floor – the *piano nobile* – up to fashion in the late 18th century.

In considering the restoration work, there were essentially two alternatives: to remove all traces of later alterations and return the house to its original form, replacing with new all missing, original features; or to retain genuine improvements or fashionable alterations carried out later in the 18th century. It is now generally accepted among experienced restoration architects that where later alterations had character or architectural significance, or where they occupy an acceptable place in the history of a building, they should be retained. Unless the integrity of the building is badly damaged, good conservation practice dictates that these should be retained. They help to tell the story of the building.

The final brief for No.17 adopted a mixture of these two approaches. The building would be restored as far as practical (taking into account current building, fire and other statutory regulations) to its early 18th-century form, retaining as much of the original material as possible, but where this was impractical, to reproduce exactly all the design features of the original. The materials employed in making these replacements would be such as could not be confused with originals. It was recognised that serious efforts had been made in the late 18th or early 19th century to bring some of the interior of the house up to contemporary standards. The room which was most extensively modernised in the late 18th century was, the first-floor drawing room. In keeping with the policy of trying to retain an example of later alterations to the building, it was decided that this was the obvious place. Virtually every decorative feature of the early 18th century had been replaced with features in fashion at a later date.

The brief also determined that the entire building would be operated as a single volume, with one use. While this restricted the options for the future use of the building, it was nonetheless decided that the importance of the building as a heritage artefact warranted this ordering of priorities.

Survey and Documentation

The first phase of the work was to document and record the condition of the building as it stood when acquired by Temple Bar Properties, before any restoration work began. This work consisted of making a measured survey of the entire building, together with a similarly detailed photographic record of all of the features of the house. On completion of this work and when the survey drawings were prepared, a structural investigation of the fabric was carried out to establish the stability of the building. At the same time as this work was being carried out, a comprehensive examination of the decorative and other features was undertaken to establish how much of the existing material could be retained and how much needed to be replaced. It was only after the preliminary stages of this investigative work was carried out that the contractors were allowed to remove material from its position for detailed examination.

Restoration

Building work began by implementing various measures to stabilise the very weak structure. Floors were propped from basement to roof, the staircase was strengthened and the building generally was made as safe as possible. Many of

the existing doors and windows were late 19th- or early 20th-century replacements, and were immediately be discarded. Fortunately, sufficient examples of the originals remained to enable the restoration to be undertaken. Recent additions and alterations – modern plaster, chipboard, hardboard partitions, etc – were removed. This revealed quite a lot of previously unknown 18th-century panelling, built-up door opes, and other clues which helped to identify changes to the original house. But it also revealed a most interesting and unexpected collection of wallpaper fragments dating from 1790 until the 1930s, a span of over 140 years. Examples of these fragments are described in a report prepared by David Skinner, an expert on historic wallpapers.

The single most important feature of this house is its almost intact early 18th-century wall panelling. Panelled houses in Dublin have virtually disappeared, and so restoring a house with this panelling almost intact was extremely important. However, much of it was in a poor state, especially that on the staircase. Elaborate bolection moulded panelling was used originally in all of the principal rooms, in the entrance hall and staircase, up to the landing between the first and second floors. From there on, the staircase was panelled in a simplified form of panelling. This was repaired and the missing sections replaced. Generally speaking, the mouldings, which were separate members applied on to the flat surface of the panel, were in good condition, although badly clogged with a couple of hundred years of oil paint. When cleaned, however, the mouldings appeared crisp and sharp.

The staircase itself was structurally very weak. Much of the supporting timber of both the staircase and the landings was badly decayed. The turned balusters, newel posts and the moulded hand rails were generally in good condition and needed little repair, apart from cleaning off centuries of oil paint. Very few were missing and in need of replacement.

Fortunately, there remained in the house many examples of original doors, so that there was no difficulty in replacing missing ones with new ones of the same pattern. Similarly, good examples of the original bolection moulded door architraves remained, and these too were reproduced and used where required. All of the window sashes surviving in the house were Victorian or later replacements. None of the original sashes of the early 18th century survived, so the architects had to choose a pattern from the windows of houses in Temple Bar of a similar date.

As in most of the smaller, early 18th-century Dublin houses, there was no decorative plasterwork apart from some simple run cornices, which sat side by side with timber ones of similar design. There is, in the entrance hall, a small, eight-leafed ceiling rose, but this is part of the late 18th-century modernisation scheme. Four chimney pieces remained in position in the house when Temple Bar Properties took possession. Three were of a very simple design and were probably original to the house. The fourth was a late 18th- or early 19th-century piece, so heavily painted with oil paint that it was impossible to determine whether it was gesso on timber or carved timber. When it was cleaned, it was discovered to be beautifully carved pine. One of the original chimney pieces was in such fragile condition that when disturbed for repair it simply fell apart. This, therefore, left two simple chimney pieces of stone and the late 18th-century carved timber chimney piece from the first-floor front room. It was decided that replacements should be made of timber, marblised, and designed in early 18th-century style to fit in with the panelling. This way, they will present the correct image, but cannot be mistaken for original ones.

The final work to be carried out to the interior was to decide on the general decoration, colour scheme and wall finish. The original colour schemes were researched by taking microscopic samples of paint from the various features of the building. The decoration scheme seen today is based on the resulting specialist's report. After much discussion with the historic wallpaper consultant, a fragment from which there was sufficient to identify the colours and discern a definite pattern was chosen. This was one of the earliest papers found, and dates from the late Georgian period (1790-1830). Celbridge Studios reproduced this paper in sufficient quantity to decorate the room as it is seen today. It was also manufactured using similar paper and techniques to those used when the paper was originally made. This completed the restoration of the interior.

Little was done to the rear elevation other than restoring the windows, door, and carrying out general repairs, including the raising of the rear parapet wall to its original height so that the east-facing windows on the top floor could be reinstated. The principal elevation to Eustace Street had, however, been badly mutilated over the years. It will be readily appreciated that the restoration of the front and the two side gables, together with the missing top floor, was essential, as these were among the main features of the house.

Certain alterations which had been made to the house could not be reversed – these included the external plastering. The surface of the brickwork had been so badly damaged prior to plastering that it could not be exposed, for both structural and aesthetic reasons. It was intended, therefore, that the existing plaster finish to the façade be repaired and retained. Unfortunately (or perhaps fortunately), the contractor misinterpreted the instructional notes on the drawings and started to hack off the existing plaster. On reaching the ground floor and removing the cement architrave around the entrance door, it was discovered that buried under the plaster were the remains of the original cut-stone doorcase. Some repairs had to be carried out, but the bones of the original doorcase had miraculously survived. The architects were further pleased to note that the design prepared on the original drawings for the restoration of this door was virtually identical with that found under the cement plaster.

T AUSTIN DUNPHY

18 EUSTACE STREET

JOHN O'CONNELL ARCHITECT

L IKE NO.17 EUSTACE STREET, NO.18 WAS ACQUIRED BY Temple Bar Properties from CIÉ in 1991. The buildings that had formerly occupied the sites of Nos.19-21 Eustace Street had been removed in the 1970s or 1980s, and the exposed gable wall of No.18 was propped with timber raking shores. The street frontage of the building is 12.8m or 30ft 7in, and thus unusually wide. The present building has replaced two earlier buildings, and this can be confirmed by comparing the Roque map of the area in 1756 with the later Ordnance Survey map of 1861. This can also be inferred by comparing No.18 with the combined sites of Nos.16 and 17 Eustace Street.

Having commissioned detailed architectural, structural, and fire safety surveys of the building, Temple Bar Properties decided to undertake its conservation for office purposes, initially for its own use as a headquarters for the life of the Temple Bar development programme.

From the style of construction, from the floor and roof timbers, and, in particular, from the design of the staircase, it is reasonable to assume that this building was constructed c.1780 to 1810, probably for semi-public uses, such as a counting house, a bank or other business premises.

The condition survey of the building showed it to be generally in a reasonable, if dilapidated, state of repair. The failure of hoppers and rain-water pipes over the years resulted in considerable water penetration of the building, in particular at first-floor level on the Eustace Street elevation.

The front elevation of No.18 Eustace Street is of brick, and is four bays wide with four storeys over basement. The back elevation was rendered approximately twenty years ago. The brickwork to the second and third floors of the front elevation had been rendered over, and, in addition, metal ties had also been installed. The door surround is in the form of an arch containing a fanlight, supported by two free-standing columns with a full entablature, all constructed of sandstone. All of the windows are up-and-down sash windows, the first floor windows being the largest, denoting that this is the main floor of the building. They are 3m high by 1.4m wide.

It was helpful to compare the condition of the building with

the earlier survey carried out by the Irish Architectural Archive in 1985, providing, for example, evidence of features which had already been removed when the building was acquired in 1991. It had been occupied until some five years previously by (variously) a gymnasium, legal stationers and artists' studios. Many of the original interior features had been damaged or replaced over time, or remodelled to change the character of the internal spaces.

A dramatic timber staircase, the main architectural feature of the building, rises from ground to the third floor. Although in poor condition, it is of considerable merit, having been skilfully designed and executed – in part cantilevered – with carved end-brackets and square timber banisters, together with mahogany handrail.

The basement had been substantially remodelled in the last twenty or thirty years, but there was a brick vault leading from a back internal court immediately behind the building. It is speculated that this served as an access from a mews, formerly located on Temple Lane, at the rear of the building.

The rooms on the first floor were among the most highly decorated, although much of the original detail – fireplaces, mouldings, cornices, chair-rails, skirting, and so forth – had been damaged or removed. The timber floor, on this and the ground floor, appeared to be a 19th-century replacement of the original.

The ground-floor plan is a somewhat more elaborate version of the standard plan used for terraced houses of the late 18th or early 19th century. It contains an entrance hall which gives access to a staircase hall, with a front and back room to the left-hand side, and a single room to the right-hand side. Whereas the form and detailed design of staircase is similar to that found in buildings of its date, what is unusual is that it is both cantilevered and it serves the ground floor to the third (top) floor, giving this space a more public scale.

At first-floor level, it is of interest that the large room overlooking Eustace Street was presumably a meeting or boardroom, while the smaller back room, interconnected with the boardroom, may have been the partner's office. It is not altogether clear if the original intention was to create a single room overlooking Eustace Street, as the chimney breast in the small room is the same size as that in the meeting or boardroom. All of the main areas at ground and first-floor level contained the original and restrained late 18th-century neoclassical stucco decorations in the form of enriched cornices and ceiling roses, while the entire building retained much of its original joinery fittings, including windows and doors. However, all of the fireplaces had been removed.

The second and third floors reflect the design of the first floor, though they were originally fitted out in a less highly decorated manner. The basement had been substantially remodelled in the past, though the stone surround to the kitchen range survived.

The timbers to the roof are also original, and it is noteworthy that the trusses, spanning from front to back, form a distance of 11.8m as there is no central valley – an unusual feature of a house at this date.

Fortunately, both interior and exterior features of the building had been listed and, in addition, the main architectural features at ground and first floor had also been listed by the planning authority, thereby limiting the damage to its many architectural features before it was acquired by Temple Bar Properties in 1991.

The approach to restoring the building was to ensure that the structure was inspected and repaired, to conserve or restore all of the original fittings and fabric of the building with the minimum remodelling, while at the same time satisfying the conditions of building and fire regulations.

Thus the elevation to Eustace Street was cleaned and repointed using the traditional tuck-pointing. This method of pointing was used in all brick building of consequence during the 18th century and during the first half of the 19th century. It is a method used to disguise the irregular form of the bricks and the irregular thickness of the pointing by inserting a narrow strip of lime putty within the main joint.

The fine door surround was repaired, though the door and frame are faithful copies of the original. All of the sash windows have been conserved, together with the original crown or spun glass where it survived.

Internally, all of the ceilings have been retained and restored where possible, and likewise all the enriched stucco work has been conserved, together with the windows, shutters, and architraves. The Portland stone floors to the entrance hall and staircase hall are a modern introduction, as this is the finish normally found in buildings of the size and date.

In order to comply with the requirements of the fire certificate, all of the internal doors are replacements, based on a pattern of the original doors and architraves. In order to overcome the problem of providing fire-safe lobbies, at first-floor level a system of inner and outer doors was adopted as this is the form usually used in buildings of this date when it was employed to give added privacy and comfort. The timber cantilevered stairs were both repaired and reinforced with steel, while the carpet was custom made by Navan Carpets, using a pattern found in an early 19th-century fragment from Fota House, Co Cork. As the choice of light-fittings for historic buildings is important within the main rooms, early 20th-century brass and cast glass electric light-fittings were obtained and installed.

The building was restored between July 1992 and February 1993.

JOHN O'CONNELL

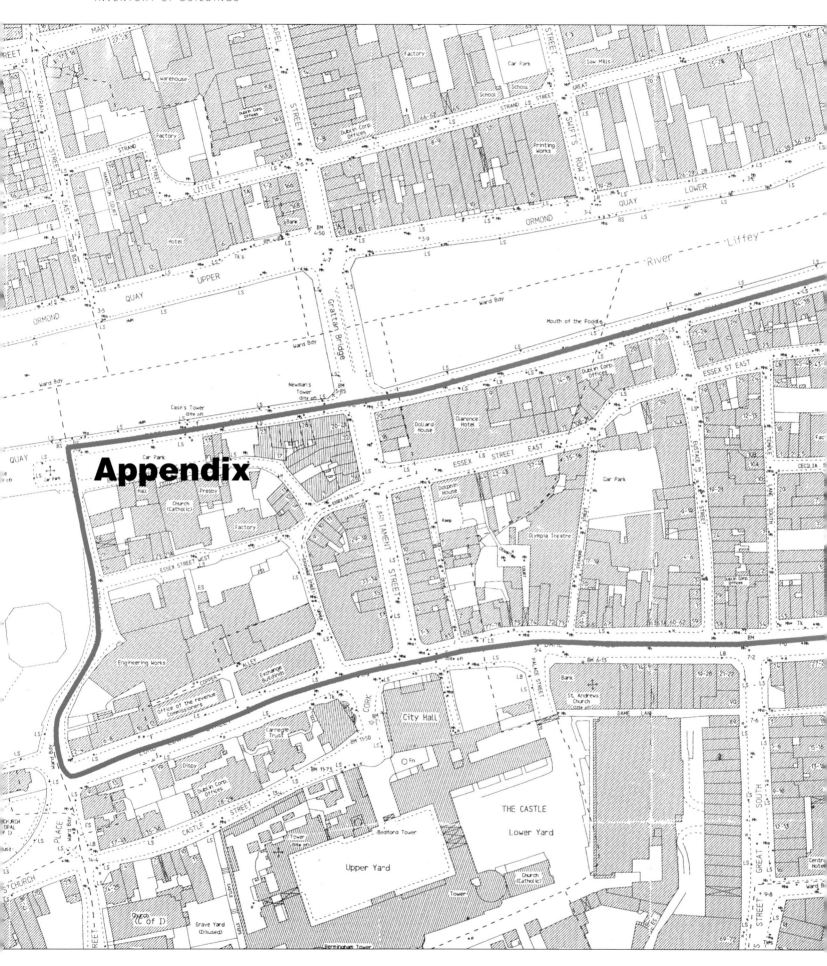

Appendix

Inventory of Buildings

The following inventory provides summary information about most construction projects in the Temple Bar area since 1991. It includes all of Temple Bar Properties' projects and the majority of private-sector developments.

All information was collated from planning applications lodged with the Planning Department at Dublin Corporation. We would like to thank the staff of the Planning Department for their kind assistance in compiling this record.

While every effort has been made to ensure that the following information is accurate at the time of publication, the publisher may not be held responsible for any errors or omissions.

COLOUR CODE

● Commercial buildings in black

● Cultural buildings in blue

● Mixed-use buildings in magenta

address	7 Anglesea Street
developer	Stephens Stephens and Traynor
completed	under construction
gross area	335m²
architects	Frank Ennis
description	Redevelopment of building as restaurant on ground floor and residential use on upper three levels.

address	1-4 Aston Quay
developer	Emer Ó Siochrú, L Enright and L Benson
completed	1994
gross area	906m²
architects	Schema
description	Refurbishment and change of use of upper floors and new penthouse extension on roof of 3-4 Aston Quay. Development comprises eight two-bedroom apartments, a maisonette and an office/studio suite, with new access from Bedford Row.

address	4-5 College Green
developer	USIT Ireland Ltd
completed	1996
gross area	1,003m²
architects	Frank Kenny Associates
description	Redevelopment of building for use as offices and retail space on ground floor.

address	1-2 Aston Place
developer	Hawkeshead Ltd
completed	1994
gross area	1526m²
architects	Frank Kenny Associates
description	The National Student Centre comprises a function room, bar/reception area, student information centre and student union office.

address	19-21 Aston Quay and 1 Price's Lane
developer	USIT Ireland Ltd
completed	1991
gross area	467m²
architects	Tritschler Tritschler and Associates
description	Redevelopment of building for offices and retail space.

address	2 Crow Street and 25 Temple Lane
developer	Temple Bar Properties
completed	1992
gross area	488m²
architects	Douglas Wallace Oppermann
description	The development of retail and restaurant uses on the ground floor and basement, and first- and second-floor use as a design studio.

address	3-4 Crow Street and 23-24 Temple Lane South
developer	Temple Bar Properties
completed	1994
gross area	1376m²
architects	Murray O'Laoire Associates
description	The Green Building is an energy-efficient development built on a gap site. It incorporates retail space on the ground floor and basement, offices on the first floor, and eight apartments on the upper three levels.

address	9 Crown Alley and 9-9a Fownes Street
developer	Temple Bar Properties
completed	1995
gross area	811m²
architects	Group 91 / Grafton Architects
description	Temple Bar Square incorporates four retail units, two restaurants and nine apartments, fronting on to a public square.

address	58 Dame Street and 29 Eustace Street
developer	RC Etchingham
completed	1994
gross area	435m²
architects	Hamilton Young & Associates
description	Redeveloped as a tourist hostel on the first and second floors, with restaurant and catering facilities on the ground floor and basement.

address	5 Crow Street
developer	Temple Bar Properties
completed	1993
gross area	113m²
architects	Róisín Murphy
description	Refurbished as a retail space on the ground floor and a one-bedroom and two-bedroom apartment on the upper floors.

address	50-52 Dame Street and 1a Crow Street
developer	Temple Bar Properties
completed	1995
gross area	1320m²
architects	Michael Collins Associates
description	50-52 Dame Street is a refurbished Georgian building incorporating twelve one-bedroom apartments and three retail units.

address	64 Dame Street and 1 Coghills Court
developer	Ciarán McGrath
completed	1995
gross area	792m²
architects	Anthony Moore
description	Development of restaurant on ground floor and ten apartments on upper floors.

address	76 Dame Street
developer	Master Credit
completed	1995
gross area	614m²
architects	M Brennan
description	Change of use from offices on the first, second and third floors to six apartments.

address	12 Essex Street East
developer	Temple Bar Properties
completed	1993
gross area	468m²
architects	Felim Dunne & Associates / Robinson Keefe Devane
description	Designyard, the applied crafts centre, was fully refurbished and incorporates jewellery gallery, furniture and commissioning galleries, offices and conference facilities.

address	24 Essex Street East
developer	Brendan McGrath
completed	1993
gross area	327.6m²
architects	Gerard Cantan
description	Development of restaurant on ground floor and three three-bedroom apartments on the upper floors.

address	80 Dame Street
developer	C & L Mohan
completed	1994
gross area	179m²
architects	Frank Kenny Associates
description	First floor refurbished as studio apartment and upper three floors as offices.

address	21-23 Essex Street East and 26-30 Wellington Quay
developer	Temple Bar Properties
completed	1995
gross area	1927m²
architects	Douglas Wallace Oppermann
description	The Cobbles incorporates 23 apartments - a mixture of newly built and refurbished - and five retail/restaurant units on the ground floor.

address	25-27 Essex Street East and 12-13 Temple Lane
developer	Temple Bar Properties
completed	1995
gross area	997m²
architects	Group 91 / Derek Tynan Architects
description	The Printworks incorporates three retail units on Essex Street East, a design studio on Temple Lane, and ten apartments on the combined upper floors.

address   26-29 Essex Street East
developer   John Morris
completed   under construction
gross area   972m²
architects   Liam Mathews and Partners
description   Refurbishment and extension
                of existing pub to include
                adjoining site at 28 Essex
                Street East, rear of 26 and 27,
                and first floor of 28 and 29.
                Three apartments will also be
                built on the second floor of
                28-29.

address   34 Essex Street East
developer   Temple Bar Properties
completed   1995
gross area   1877m²
architects   Group 91 /
                O'Donnell and Tuomey
description   The Gallery of Photography is a
                newly built exhibition space
                incorporating darkrooms,
                offices and a gallery, fronting
                on to Meeting House Square.

address   Eustace Street, Essex Street
                East and Sycamore Street
developer   Temple Bar Properties
completed   1996
gross area   800m²
architects   Group 91 /
                Paul Keogh Architects
description   Meeting House Square is an
                open-air performance area
                bounded by four cultural
                buildings: The Ark, Gallery of
                Photography, Gaiety School of
                Acting and Photographic
                Centre.

address   31-32 Essex Street East and
                rear of 30 Essex Street East
developer   Temple Bar Properties
completed   1996
gross area   1877m²
architects   Group 91 /
                O'Donnell and Tuomey
description   Built on a gap site, the National
                Photography Centre houses
                the DIT School of Photography
                and the National Photographic
                Archive. Incorporated are
                lecture theatres, darkrooms,
                student facilities and a gallery.

address   3 Essex Gate, 22-23 Parliament
                Street and 23-28 Essex Quay
developer   Temple Bar Properties
completed   1996
gross area   3822m²
architects   Gilroy McMahon
description   Isolde's Tower is a mixed-use
                development, built around an
                internal courtyard, with a
                restaurant and pub on Essex
                Gate, two retail units on
                Parliament Street and Essex
                Quay, and 35 apartments on
                the upper floors.

address   6 Eustace Street
developer   Temple Bar Properties
completed   1993
gross area   2810m²
architects   O'Donnell and Tuomey
description   Redevelopment of Friends
                Meeting House as Irish Film
                Centre, incorporating two
                cinemas, bar, restaurant and
                offices. The Irish Film Archive is
                also based at the IFC.

address	9-10 Eustace Street
developer	Glora Investments
completed	1996
gross area	790m²
architects	Scott Tallon Walker
description	Refurbishment of building to be used as restaurant on basement level and local property management office on the upper floors.

address	11a Eustace Street
developer	Temple Bar Properties
completed	1995
gross area	1600m²
architects	Group 91 / Shane O'Toole and Michael Kelly
description	Refurbishment of the 18th-century Presbyterian Meeting House as the Ark, a cultural centre for children, with theatre, dressing rooms, studio, workshop, exhibition spaces and offices.

address	17 Eustace Street
developer	Temple Bar Properties
completed	1995
gross area	302m²
architects	Dunphy O'Connor Baird
description	17 Eustace Street is a four-storey-over-basement building, refurbished to original 18th-century specifications, to be used as an enterprise and information centre.

address	11 Eustace Street
developer	Temple Bar Properties
completed	1996
gross area	1500m²
architects	Group 91 / Shane O'Toole and Michael Kelly
description	The ground floor and basement have been developed as a pedestrian archway between Eustace Street and Meeting House Square, with artists' studios on the upper floors.

address	15 Eustace Street
developer	Temple Bar Properties
completed	1996
gross area	316m²
architects	Derek Tynan Architects
description	Redevelopment of restaurant on ground floor and information centre for Focus Point housing advice centre.

address	18 Eustace Street
developer	Temple Bar Properties
completed	1992
gross area	695m²
architects	John O'Connell
description	18 Eustace Street is a four-storey-over-basement building, refurbished as offices to original 18th-century specifications. Currently it is the offices of Temple Bar Properties, with the Temple Bar Information Centre on the ground floor.

address	19-21 Eustace Street and 7-9 Temple Lane South
developer	Temple Bar Properties
completed	1996
gross area	192m²
architects	Group 91 / Shay Cleary Architects
description	Curved Street is bound by Arthouse, the multi-media centre for the arts, and Temple Bar Music Centre. It was built on a gap site on Eustace Street and a disused warehouse on Temple Lane South.

address	Exchange Buildings, 16-18 Lord Edward Street
developer	Regan Developments Ltd
completed	Proposed completion: 1997
gross area	2750m²
architects	JM Moran
description	Development of new third floor, and conversion of building to hotel, restaurant and ancillary facilities.

address	11-15 Fishamble Street
developer	USIT Ireland
completed	1996
gross area	N/A
architects	Tritschler Tritschler and Associates
description	The Harding Hotel is a new 55-bedroom hotel with restaurant and bar, developed on the site of a disused warehouse.

address	23-24 Eustace Street and 4 Temple Lane
developer	Juilleard Ltd
completed	1995
gross area	822m²
architects	Frank Kenny
description	The River House Hotel is a 29-bedroom hotel incorporating Danger Doyle's bar and the Mission nightclub.

address	7 Lower Exchange Street and 16-18 Essex Street
developer	Temple Bar Properties
completed	1996
gross area	3,387m²
architects	Gilroy McMahon
description	Former SS Michael & John's church and schools have been redeveloped as Dublin's Viking Adventure – a multi-media exhibition space on one of Dublin's primary Viking locations.

address	13-17 Fleet Street and 16a Adair Lane
developer	Rainbow Electronics
completed	1994
gross area	4037m²
architects	Design and Management
description	The Temple Bar Hotel is a 108-bedroom hotel, with function room in the basement, and ground floor as reception, restaurant and bar.

address	19-20 Fleet Street, 12 Westmoreland Street and 4-5 Price's Lane
developer	Bewleys Delgado Ltd
completed	1995
gross area	3590m²
architects	Paul Brazil
description	Redevelopment of premises as 70-bedroom Bewley's hotel, incorporating bar, restaurant, café and shop.

address	Fleet Street, Anglesea Street, Parliament Row and Foster Place
developer	Lowstrand Properties
completed	1995
gross area	13,418m²
architects	Anthony Cotter
description	Development of multi-storey car-park, with one retail unit and restaurant on Fleet Street and a tourist hostel on Anglesea Street.

address	3-5 Fownes Street Upper
developer	Imelda O'Donnell
completed	1995
gross area	774m²
architects	Lisney Building Surveyors
description	Development and restoration of listed buildings as retail space on ground floor, and upper floors as one apartment.

address	57-58 Fleet Street
developer	Slattery's
completed	1994
gross area	755m²
architects	Pat Dargan
description	Redevelopment of existing bar to include restaurant and function room.

address	1 Fownes Street Upper and 18 Crow Street
developer	Urillo Ltd
completed	under construction
gross area	447m²
architects	Douglas Wallace
description	Redevelopment of existing Foggy Dew pub on ground floor and basement level to include adjoining building on 18 Crow Street, and conversion of upper levels on Fownes Street as two apartments.

address	6-7 Fownes Street Upper and 9-19 Crow Street
developer	Temple Bar Properties
completed	1995
gross area	2810m²
architects	Burke Kennedy Doyle
description	Spranger's Yard incorporates 23 apartments, a mixture of newly built and refurbished, around a raised internal courtyard and 13 retail units on the ground floor.

address	11 Fownes Street Upper
developer	Sé Sí Ltd
completed	1993
gross area	136m²
architects	Padraig McHugh
description	Development of derelict building as retail space on ground floor and basement, and a one-bedroom apartment.

address	5-7 Parliament Street
developer	Temple Bar Properties / ODC
completed	1992
gross area	1446m²
architects	Schema
description	Formerly the Royal Exchange Hotel, this was the first major development with a significant residential element to come on the market after the Temple Bar legislation was enacted in 1991. It consists of 15 apartments on three floors, and three retail units on street level.

address	27-28 Parliament Street
developer	Dublin Taverns
completed	1995
gross area	1641m²
architects	Steven Byrne Architects
description	Redevelopment of building as the Turk's Head Chop House restaurant, bar and café was completed in 1995. The upper floors will be developed as a hotel.

address	1-3 Parliament Street and 81-82 Dame Street
developer	Hugh O'Regan
completed	1995
gross area	1162m²
architects	Murray O'Laoire
description	Redeveloped as Thomas Read's restaurant and bar on ground floor and basement level, with ten apartments on the upper floors.

address	16-18 Parliament Street
developer	Iskasinc Ltd
completed	1996
gross area	632m²
architects	Frank Ennis
description	Development of existing premises at No.18 and gap site at Nos.16 and 17 as Porter House multi-leisure facility, incorporating bar, micro-brewery and restaurant.

address	33-34 Parliament Street and 3-6 Upper Exchange Street
developer	Temple Bar Properties
completed	1995
gross area	2650m²
architects	Campbell Conroy Hickey
description	The Cutlers is a development of 23 apartments with parking in the basement and The Front Lounge on the ground floor.

address	35 Parliament Street
developer	Colm Ó Siochrú
completed	1992
gross area	362m²
architects	Colm Ó Siochrú
description	The development consists of a restaurant at basement and ground-floor levels, and four apartments on the upper floors.

address	10-14 Sycamore Street
developer	Temple Bar Properties
completed	1995
gross area	1300m²
architects	Group 91 / Paul Keogh Architects
description	The Sycamore Building incorporates a bar/restaurant space on the ground floor and the Gaiety School of Acting on the upper floors.

address	4-5 Temple Bar
developer	Temple Bar Properties
completed	1994
gross area	465m²
architects	McCullough Mulvin
description	The Black Church Print Studio is a refurbished building incorporating a print studio on the upper three floors and a gallery on the ground floor and mezzanine.

address	37-40 Parliament Street and 1-6 Cork Hill
developer	PJ McGrath
completed	1993
gross area	743m²
architects	Tritschler Tritschler & Assoc
description	4-5 Cork Hill is a retail unit, while 1-2 Cork Hill, at basement and ground-floor levels, was refurbished as a restaurant space. The upper floors of 1-6 Cork Hill, including 37 Parliament Street, have been refurbished as apartments and offices.

address	3 Temple Bar and 33 Wellington Quay
developer	Maridor Developments Ltd
completed	under construction
gross area	521m²
architects	Ambrose Kelly Group
description	Development of gap site at 3 Temple Bar and adjoining building on 33 Wellington Quay as seven one-bedroom apartments over two retail units on ground floor.

address	5-9 Temple Bar and 37-39 Wellington Quay
developer	Temple Bar Properties
completed	1994
gross area	2121.5m²
architects	McCullough Mulvin
description	The existing Temple Bar Gallery and Studios was fully refurbished and extended to include 9 Temple Bar. It houses 22 artists' studios on the upper floors and a gallery on the ground floor.

Inventory of Public Art

Temple Bar Properties has, from the beginning, incorporated the work of visual artists into its development programme, whether in the form of street furniture, temporary work in gap sites or vacant buildings, specially designed hoardings around projects under construction, or permanent works in new buildings or public spaces.

The list below itemises these artistic interventions. To the best of our knowledge, it is correct at the time of going to press.

Róisín de Buitléar
Untitled 1996
DIT School of Photography (wall installation)
Glass, steel cladding, 350 x 40 x 30cm

'The concept is inspired by viewfinders, lenses and shapes made by scattered photographs on a table. Layers of blown, coloured glass fragments were cast within a mould to form solid blocks of glass, which, in turn, were hot-formed and fitted into the cavity wall. When the coloured glass blocks are overlapped, the light is diffused and a third colour emerges. '

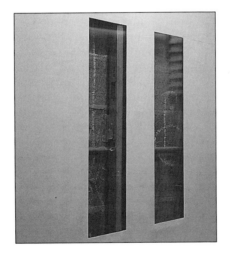

Gerard Byrne
Untitled, 1996
Temple Bar Music Centre
Glass, mirrors

This is series of transparent glass installations and mirrors in various locations throughout the building. The glass reveals the physical substructure and the mechanical and electrical services which are normally not seen.

Maud Cotter
Absolute Jellies Make Singing Sounds, 1994
The Green Building
Found/recycled glass, oak, steel, copper, aluminium, brass, iron, plastics, 5 x 2.2m

The double-height door and surrounds (on Temple Lane) celebrate the innate aesthetic value of discarded items, framed in steel, and visible, in part, both on the inside and the outside of the building. The door acts both as an artwork and a functioning door, conforming with the building's technical specifications.

Sarah Daly
Mosaic River, 1993
Designyard
Broken ceramic - approx. 8 x 1m

The work is a response to the brief to mark
the location of the River Poddle, which flows
beneath the building. The colours and curving
line of the work are intended to soften the
otherwise minimal and monotone character of
the Jewellery Gallery floor area. It also has the
effect of leading the public into the back of
the building, through to the covered yard area
at the rear.

Andy Folan
Intaglio, 1995
Black Church Print Studio (door to studios)
Cast bronze, wood, coloured glass, film,
2.85 x 1.7m

'The ink transfer process of intaglio printing
was the inspiration for this work. During
printing, paper is moulded into the hollows of
the etched plate which contains ink. Peeling
the print from the plate is the moment that
intaglio attempts to capture. The image was
inspired by a greatly enlarged photograph of
an insect wing.

Rachel Joynt
Film Reel, 1994
Irish Film Centre
Stainless steel with brass insets,
diameter 38cm

Set into a granite paving stone, *Film Reel* was
commissioned to signal the entrance to the
Irish Film Centre. The artist worked from an
old film reel in the film archive in designing
the work.

Felim Egan
Untitled, 1996
Meeting House Square
Lead, steel, glass

While the work is located on three sites, it is
conceived as one installation, relating to the
structures and features of the building and the
archway. The lead-clad wall over the
archway, facing on to Meeting House Square,
is the largest and most dramatic aspect of the
work. In all the pieces, the glass insets will
glow with light during daylight hours, and
become dramatic with dusk and darkness.

Remco de Fouw
The Tree of Life, 1994
The Green Building
Recycled copper cistern tanks, taps, pipes
and other found objects, 5 x 2.2m

The double-height door and surrounds (on
Crow Street) are a response to the concept of
the building itself – the integration of
environmentally friendly technologies into the
built environment. The materials used are all
recycled, and the techniques used in making
the work were sensitive to energy
conservation.

John Kindness
*Teething troubles in an energy-
efficient restaurant*, 1995
ESB sub-station gates
Steel, enamel, 2.4 x 2.2m

The brief was to mask the ESB sub-station
whilst complying with the relevant ESB
technical standards. Given the free-standing
nature of this installation, enamel – a material
capable of withstanding the wear and tear of
urban activity – was chosen. The brief and the
sub-station's proximity to the Green Building
were the direct inspiration for the image.

James Scanlon
Under A Low Sun, 1996
The Ark (basement ceiling)
Mild steel, patinated copper, etched flashed glass, plasterboard, 15.2 x 3m

Under a low sun / The band is marching now
Past the painted doors
And down along the promenade,
Toward the cold shore and turning
Until all the wind-snatched silver life strikes
Bright against the tide:
And after / Come the marching children,
Growing smaller and smaller
In their uniforms
— Moya Cannon, Narrow Gatherings, 1990

Darrell Viner
In Sight, 1995
Temple Bar Gallery and Studios
Lights, electrical circuits

The idea of *In Sight* is to reflect the ongoing activities within the building. The use of the lift is signalled at roof level with four white lamps. As the lift moves from floor to floor, different combinations of lamps light up. The use of water in the studios is indicated by four lights placed at roof level, above the artists' entrance. Lights set into the pavement outside pulse at different speeds in relation to the use of electricity throughout the building.

James Scanlon
Waterline, 1996
The Ark (windows to Meeting House Square)
Etched flashed glass, 1 window, 48 x 47.5cm; 5 windows, each 18 x 22.5cm
(1 window illustrated)

Kathy Prendergast
Untitled, 1993
Designyard
Wrought iron, four opes – each 3.25 x 1.05m

The gates are inspired by the fact that the shape and character of cities are formed by their rivers. The four cities represented are Dublin, Madrid, New York and Vienna. The gates were made in Dublin to the artist's design by a third-generation blacksmith, Harry Page. The highly tactile surface of the finished gates reveals the hammer strokes of the blacksmith.

Grace Weir
Untitled, 1996
Dublin's Viking Adventure (south & east walls)
Glass-reinforced fibre with bronze insets

'This work is based on the history of the immediate area, which would have been the quay area where the Vikings moored their longboats. The work layers depictions of these historical events, using diagrammatical drawings of a longboat, with maps of the position of the stars during spring 998, and drawings from weather isobar charts, layered over images of clouds and the sea.'

Blue Funk
(V Connor, T Green, K Hardy, J Irvine, K Kelly)
Well Camera Lamp, 1992
temporary installation, Eustace Street

Helen Bolger
Railing Seat, 1992
street furniture, Eustace Street Lower

Helen Bolger
An Organ of Flight, 1994
sculptural Christmas tree, Temple Bar Square

Michael Boran
Citizens, 1992
temporary installation, Essex Street East

Vincent Browne
The Palm Tree, 1992
street furniture, Temple Bar

Vincent Browne
Mirrored Helix, 1994
sculptural Christmas tree, Temple Bar Square

Róisín de Buitléar
Christmas Baubles, 1994
sculptural Christmas tree, Temple Bar Square

Eoin Byrne
Something From Nothing, 1992
temporary installation, 12 Essex Street East

Evelyn Byrne
Well Camera Lamp, 1992
temporary installation, Eustace Street

Rhona Byrne, Barbara Ellison & Nessa Ryan
Cooker Ring Curtain, 1993
5 Crow Street

Cathy Carman
There's a woman there whose wounds cry out like stones from a sling, 1992
temporary installation, 5 Temple Bar

Cathy Carman
Untitled work, 1992
temporary installation, Essex Street East

Cathy Carman
My Heart, My Grove of Nuts, 1992
temporary installation, Essex Street East

Cathy Carman
Holly Head, 1994
sculptural Christmas tree, Temple Bar Square

Brian Connolly & Maurice O'Connell
Gateways, 1994
temporary installation at Temple Bar perimeter

Maeve Connolly
Untitled, 1993
temporary work on hoarding, Viking scheme, Exchange Street Lower

Maeve Connolly
Smile, 1994
sculptural Christmas tree, Temple Bar Square

Rachel Galligan & Alannah Robins
Sail Curtain, 1993
5 Crow Street

James Garner
Balcony, balustrades & gate, 1994
cladding to oval columns for the Green Building

James Garner
The Northern Alloy Star, 1994
sculptural Christmas tree, Temple Bar Square

Ronan Halpin & Paki Smith
The Wounded King, 1992
temporary installation, 9 Temple Bar

Lisa Harmey
Patches, 1993
temporary work on hoarding, Spranger's Yard scheme, Cecilia Street & Crow Street

Lisa Harmey
Ball with Flame, 1994
sculptural Christmas tree, Temple Bar Square

Peter Jones
Owl Man, 1994
sculptural Christmas tree, Temple Bar Square

Peter Jones & Aideen Lynch
Hand Shadow Images, 1993
temporary work on hoarding, The Ark scheme, 11a Eustace Street

Rachel Joynt
Cobble Piece, 1989
Cobble stones, each 25.5 x 10cm

Brian Kennedy
Stones in Place, 1992
temporary installation, 31-32 Essex Street East

Mirjam Keune
Metal Fireplace, 1993
5 Crow Street

Mirjam Keune
Little Star, 1994
sculptural Christmas tree, Temple Bar Square

David Kinnane
Untitled, 1993
temporary work on hoarding, Designyard, 12 Essex Street East

Stephen Lawlor
The Hollow Empire, 1992
temporary installation, Temple Lane South

Aideen Lynch
Christmas Globe, 1994
sculptural Christmas tree, Temple Bar Square

Gwen McCarthy
And Walls Came Tumbling Down, 1993
temporary work on hoarding, Temple Bar Square

Brian McDonald
Exit signs, 1994
The Green Building

Conor McGarrigle
Untitled, 1993
temporary work on hoarding, The Green Building, 3-4 Crow Street & 23-24 Temple Lane

Conor McGarrigle
Mobile, 1994
sculptural Christmas tree, Temple Bar Square

Joe McGill
Stations, 1992
temporary installation, 17-18 Essex Street East

Aileen MacKeogh
Untitled, 1994
sculptural Christmas tree, Temple Bar Square

Anna MacLeod
Cord, 1992
temporary installation, 21 Essex Street East (pre The Cobbles)

Betty Maguire
Historic Seat, 1992
street furniture, Fownes Street

John Moore
Beacon, 1992
temporary installation, 12 Essex Street East (pre The Cobbles)

John Moore
Teddy Angel, 1994
sculptural Christmas tree, Temple Bar Square

Janet Mullarney
One of Many Tactics, 1992
temporary installation, Essex Street East

Janet Mullarney
Maybe they are following a star?, 1994
sculptural Christmas tree, Temple Bar Square

Paul O'Reilly
Portraits, 1993
temporary work on hoarding, The Printworks
scheme, 25-27 Essex Street East, & The
Cobbles scheme, 21-23 Essex Street East

Kathy Prendergast
Oh Jesus, 1994
sculptural Christmas tree, Temple Bar Square

Alannah Robins
Tangley Chimes, 1994
sculptural Christmas tree, Temple Bar Square

Vivienne Roche
Atrium Duct, 1994
The Green Building

David Sisk
Modern Glass, 1993
5 Crow Street

Paki Smith
Sculptural Christmas treT,
Temple Bar Square

Paki Smith
Burning Boot, 1994
sculptural Christmas tree, Temple Bar Square

Marek Staskiwictz
Untitled, 1993
temporary work on hoarding, Meeting House
Square, 31-33 Essex Street East

Cléa van der Grijn
Temple Bar Distorted, 1993
temporary work on hoarding, Welllington Hotel
scheme, 17-18 Essex Street East

Cléa van der Grijn
Christmas Bells, 1994
sculptural Christmas tree, Temple Bar Square

Corban Walker
Wow it must be hot in there, 1993
temporary work on hoarding, Curved Street
scheme

Felim Egan
Untitled, 1996
Meeting House Square

219

Members of the board of Temple Bar Properties, 1991-1996

Temple Bar Properties was established by the Government in 1991, under the Temple Bar Area Renewal and Development Act.

The company is incorporated under the Companies Acts, and has one shareholder. From 1991-1993 the shareholder was the Taoiseach, and since March 1993 the shareholder has been the Minister for the Environment.

The Chairman, Pat Kenny, and all of the members of the board are appointed by the shareholder. The titles of executive directors and the positions held are shown in parentheses.

Derek Brady 1991-
Caroline Brady 1996-
Gillian Bowler 1991-1996
Peter Cassells 1991-1996
John Cullen 1993-1995
Sean Haughey 1991-1996
Owen Hickey (Property Director 1991-1996) 1991-1996
Richard Kearney 1991-1992
Pat Kenny 1991-
Philip King 1996-
Laura Magahy (Managing Director 1992-) 1991-
Anne Mathews 1996-
Caroline McCamley 1996-
Michael McNulty 1991-1996
Joseph Moreau 1991-
Tony Murray 1996-
John O'Connor 1995-
Patricia O'Donovan 1996-
Patricia Quinn (Cultural Director 1992-) 1992-
Paddy Teahon (Managing Director 1991-1992) 1991-1993
Mary Walsh 1991-1996

Sheila Byrne (Company Secretary 1991-1993)
Eve-Anne Cullinan (Company Secretary 1993-)

Selected Bibliography

Temple Bar – A Policy for its Future
Peter Pearson (ed.)
(An Taisce, Dublin, 1985)

*Temple Bar Study
– A Reappraisal of the Area and the
Proposed Central Bus Station*
Una Sugrue (ed.)
(Temple Bar Study, Dublin, 1986)

The Temple Bar Area – Action Plan
(Dublin Corporation, 1990)

Temple Bar Pilot Project
(Dublin Corporation, 1990)

*Temple Bar Lives ! #1 – The Winning
Architectural Framework Plan*
Jobst Graeve (ed.)
(TBP, Dublin, 1991)
ISBN 1-874202-00-1

*Temple Bar Lives ! #2
– A Record of the Architectural
Framework Competition*
Jobst Graeve (ed.)
(Temple Bar Properties, Du Dublin,
1991) ISBN 1-874202-01-X

*Development Programme for
Temple Bar*
Eve-Anne Cullinan (ed.)
(TBP, Dublin, 1993)
ISBN 1-874202-05-2

Excavations at Isolde's Tower, Dublin
Linzi Simpson
(TBP, Dublin, 1994)
ISBN 1-874202-06-0

*Excavations at Essex Street West,
Dublin*
Linzi Simpson
(TBP, Dublin, 1995)
ISBN 1-874202-07-9

Excavation at 33-34 Parliament Street
G Scally
(TBP, Dublin, 1996) IS

*Temple Bar – Dublin,
An Illustrated History*
Pat Liddy
(TBP, Dublin, 1992)
ISBN 1-874202-04-4 hb / -03-6 pb

*Smock Alley Theatre:
The Evolution of a Building*
Linzi Simpson
(TBP, Dublin, 1996)
ISBN 1-874202-078-7

Temple Bar – The Power of an Idea
Patricia Quinn (ed.)
(TBP, Dublin, 1996)
ISBN 1-874202-09-5

In preparation

The Archaeology of Temple Bar East,
M Gowen with M Reid
(TBP, Dublin, 1996) I)

PHOTOGRAPHIC CREDITS

New photography for this book by John Searle, with additional photography by Bill Hastings (cover), Peter Barrow (aerial), and Gerry Hayden (line drawings).

Other photographs by:

Michael Boran
M Durand
Gerry Farrell
Bill Hastings, ARC
Tim Kovar
John Searle

and from the archives of:

Gandon Archive, Kinsale
Irish Architectural Archive
Temple Bar Properties

Index